**Alistair Noakes** first started
with an old set of hickory club. ....... it was later pointed
out to him that they were made by the five-time Open
Champion J. H. Taylor, a seed was sown and a challenge
laid down: to discover more about the heritage of the game
and of those who had played it over hundreds of years.

He is a member of The Royal Liverpool Golf Club Village
Play where he enjoys playing as an artisan over the famous
Hoylake links, just a mile or so from his home. He continues
to indulge his passion for golf's rich history through his
membership of the British Golf Collectors Society.

To Paul

Happy Golfing

Best wishes

Alistair

'I found the book both informative and absorbing with a story to compliment the facts. Congratulations on an excellent tale.'

John Ball
Closest living relative to the champion golfer

## Also by Alistair Noakes

*Golf in the Soul*

available from:
www.alistairnoakes.bigcartel.com

# HOYLAKE HERO

The remarkable story of John Ball,
Britain's greatest amateur golfer

ALISTAIR NOAKES

First published in 2018

Cover photo of John Ball by Herbert Bickerton

A CIP catalogue record for this book is available from the British Library

ISBN 978-1-912804-16-0

Printed and bound in Great Britain by Biddles, Norfolk.

To Marianthi

Without whose love, encouragement and support
Hoylake Hero would never have been written.

# Contents

# A Chance Discovery

The donkeys had been braying all night to the point where even Johnny had had enough. The weather had been foul from the wee small hours and they were longing for their feed.

Johnny Ball had kept a menagerie of farm animals for much of his life. These were two of his favourites. He walked over to the gate with his bag of feed and they tussled amongst themselves for the lion's share of the spoils. There was little that gave Johnny greater pleasure than to walk through the paddocks checking on the health of his livestock.

Few knew him as a farmer, but farming was what he had chosen as his profession, that was until his later years, when he became a hotel proprietor. Most knew him as a man with a much rarer talent. It was one that had set him apart from all the rest and which had brought him much acclaim. He had become a golfer, an amateur golfer and the greatest his country had ever known. No one in their lifetime would likely match his haul of medals.

Today in the 21st century there is good money to be made from golf but over 100 years ago, in Johnny's era, there was little choice but to look elsewhere for one's livelihood. He needed the income from his farm to make his living. His whole life had been rooted in the earth, in haymaking and in tending to his cobs. When not working the land he was equally at home playing on it, striking a small ball, battling the winds and laying waste to his adversaries on the fairways of the greatest courses in the land.

He was married now. It was 1936. He had tied the knot only a few years ago with Nellie his housekeeper. In these, the autumn years of his life he was quite content whiling away his time on his small freeholding at Lygan-y-Wern, near Holywell in North Wales. On a clear day he could look across the mouth of the River Dee to his hometown of Hoylake and could just make out The Royal Hotel, the place where he'd grown up and which once housed the clubhouse to one of the greatest golf clubs in the world.

When he first started playing as a child, the sheep acted as greenkeepers and the rabbits kept the fairways tight and unpredictable. Now a small army of green staff tended to every succulent blade and the putting surfaces were as smooth as any in the land.

The rain had turned almost horizontal as he emptied out the half-full bag of feed. He wouldn't tarry here long and within a few minutes he was back inside the shed delving in amongst the drawers for a torch with which to search for a replacement sack. He muttered to himself briefly as he did so, cursing his forgetfulness for mislaying the item.

'It's got to be in here somewhere. I'm sure I left it in this drawer here.'

The light was dim and his eyesight poor, not what it used to be, but just as he was about to give up a glint of light almost dazzled him. At first he thought it was the torch itself as it shone its last rays of fading life from the overused batteries, but then he was unsure. His hands rummaged further into the recesses of the tired cabinet drawer. He pulled something out. It was a hunk of metal with a faded ribbon attached. Gently he cupped it in his hands, took it into the kitchen and turned on the light.

It was as clear as daylight now. No mere hunk of metal this. It was one of his old golf medals and not just any old medal at that. Oval in shape and still shining in its gold finery, in clear, bold lettering he could still easily make out the words stamped around the edge, 'Open Champion Trophy'.

For a second he was taken aback and was thankful for the chair that happened to be stationed behind him. He hesitated briefly and slumped backwards forcing the legs to skid on the surface of the wooden floor. He had won that medal back in 1890 at the age of 28. At the time he was the first amateur to win the Open Championship. To this day there are only three who have ever done so. How the years had drifted by. How he had played, how…. He was quite overcome. It was unusual for him. He had never been prone to such emotion, not in any obvious way but for once circumstance had got the better of him.

It was a full half an hour later before his wife came and found him.

'Nellie, look what I've just discovered,' he called out.

She felt sure she caught the faint trace of a tear in his eye but she couldn't be certain. In the dim light of the kitchen he approached her and handed her the medal. It hadn't seen the light of day for well over 40 years. He turned away. He needed some space. In truth he was a little ashamed to be showing such emotion. Slowly he walked out past his favourite oak and up onto the lawn opposite. The rain had cleared by now and shafts of golden evening light were clearly picking out the contours of the green fields that swept down to the coast.

Within a few moments Nellie was on the lawn by his side. She linked her arm in his. The donkeys were still braying. They knew they had been short-changed in their feed this morning but they were silent to Johnny's ears, for now at least.

'That's where it all started Nellie, over there in that hotel opposite.' He reached for her hand and tightened his grip. 'I was only a young lad when I first started playing. I can remember it to this very day....'

# A Young Boy's Curiosity

A head appeared from around the corner of the banisters in the grand stairway of The Royal Hotel. It was that of seven year old Johnny Ball who like any young child, wanted to be part of the action. Upstairs tucked up in bed were his five sisters – Elisabeth, Margaret, Annie, Katherine and Ada. Together they shared three of the many bedrooms in this grand old Georgian building. Carefully, Johnny sneaked down the steps and hid behind one of the pillars which acted as main support to this magnificent building.

The large bar room at The Royal Hotel was much busier than normal. Behind the counter Johnny could just make out the tall figure of his father, John Ball Senior, an imposing, athletic man who revelled in the attention that came with being the hotel's tenant landlord. Even at this distance Johnny could hear his fulsome voice as it rose above the level of the general bar room chatter. As ever his father was doing all that he could to ensure a convivial evening's entertainment was being laid on for those who entered. This evening though, he was pushing the boat out.

Further to his left Johnny spotted his mother, Margaret, busy directing the team of attractive waitresses dispensing drinks to the more well-to-do clients over in the corner. Voices were being raised. Johnny had heard his mother and father talking earlier in the day. They were expecting a big crowd and had ordered in extra supplies for their many guests, and at considerable expense. But who were they and why were they coming? He was eager to find out.

No one had noticed him as he mingled in the crowd. He was anonymous to most, but he was still keen to hide his presence from his parents. He turned to his right and entered the main bar room itself. In front of him a fire crackled away and flames licked up the tall chimney breast bouncing the heat back into the room. Within seconds it became too overwhelming and he moved away. In a small gap between the bodies in front of him, his eyes were drawn to the portrait up on the wall. It was that of Lord Stanley of Alderley. Lord Stanley owned the hotel and much of the land around Hoylake including the large expanse of sandy wasteland opposite, known as the warren. With a few exceptions, he was well liked in these parts and was aided by his convivial tenant landlord, John Ball Senior, Johnny's father, who charged prices that met with the approval of most who entered the hotel.

Johnny had never paid any real attention to the painting before despite his father's explanations but tonight the flames seemed to pick out the proud face of the man quite clearly. His look was stern and Johnny cowered at first as the light caught the whites of his eyes. It reminded him of his intimidating headmaster and when the orangey glow from the fire caught the red of his jacket the portrait took on a more menacing feel. It was as if the man himself was taking an ever more watchful eye and listening ear to all that was happening in the bars of this most respectful hotel.

Hoylake had got its name from the Hoyle Lake - a becalmed sea lake protected by the sandy Hoyle Bank a mile or so offshore. Boats would use the lake to anchor up before preparing to enter the Mersey and the Liverpool docks. In previous times it had proved such a safe anchorage that William III had used it as an embarkation port for his 10,000 troops en route to Ireland to fight in the Battle of the Boyne. Sadly in recent years the estuarine lake had begun to silt up and the number of fishing stacks had dwindled considerably. Despite this a few small masts still bobbed offshore and their owners from the likes of the Becks and Eccles families would row their smaller boats ashore to take in the pleasures of the many bars and pubs of Hoylake. On nights after good catches the beer flowed and the songs that were sung were bold and joyful. Their voices had impressed the ears of this young lad before but tonight they were silent. Tonight there were other gentlemen present who had caught Johnny's eye.

To his right Johnny couldn't help but notice a stout, imperious man whose moustache seemed to stretch the full width of his face. In lieu of the customary cigarette, a fat cigar was being gently chewed from the corner of his mouth, a process in which he seemed to take great pleasure. Johnny watched as the gentleman took a match from a silver vesta case and after several failed strikes, he finally succeeded in bringing the object to life. In the few moments that followed Johnny lost all sight of his man. As the cloud of heady smoke engulfed the gentleman's face Johnny was forced to retreat. When he reappeared once again, his true colours were there to be admired. Covering his ample girth he sported a lightly checked tweed jacket. Underneath, a smart cravat encircled his neck. To his left and propped up against the windowsill stood a dark, handsome cane, topped by a silver decorated handle. There was certainly

7

something different about this chap, Johnny thought. He was intrigued. Why was he here? Was he one of the invited guests he had overheard his father talking about?

With these thoughts still lingering in Johnny's mind, a second man of similar stature and attire approached from the opposite corner of the room. This gentleman sported a double-breasted suit with matching regal hat. He greeted his friend as if they were long lost cousins. Within minutes heads were turned as their loud conversation filled the room. When Mr. John Dunn spoke people listened.

From the corner of his eye Johnny caught the gaze of his mother. He wasn't sure whether she had spotted him or not. The smoke was thick and the visibility poor but whichever way, it was time for him to move on. He ducked down and skirted round the corner nearly crashing into one of the tables to his right. Steady now, take it easy, he thought. If I move further over here now, I can't be seen. Maybe behind that pillar? That's good. Take a breath. I'm safe here for the moment, but just be careful.

Relieved to be hidden from view for the time being, Johnny scanned the colourful scene before him. People were coming and going from every direction. Some were proudly attired in silk waistcoats with pocket watches dangling from chains. Others smoked cigars or pipes hiding expensive cravats that oozed opulence in the extreme. From the far corner of the room the blue-jerseyed fishermen eyed these gentlemen with equal curiosity.

A flash from his right made Johnny look up. The fire was coming to life again and the reflection from the grandly decorated mirror behind had left him on view once more to his parents serving at the bar. Carefully he moved to his left and found a stool in the corner. Here he could melt away and be hidden from familiar eyes. He was treading a fine line but it was worth it. Such comings and goings rarely happened at The Royal Hotel and he was intrigued by all he saw.

As the evening wore on, the bar became busier and busier. More distinguished people entered. One man sporting reddish whiskers and a magnificent ginger beard, the sum of which more than made up for the lack of hair on his head, was so actively engrossed in his animated conversation that more of the contents of his whisky glass were hitting the floor than were ever likely to end up down his throat. Mr. James Muir Dowie liked his drink and conversation.

It was now 8.30pm and things were beginning to happen. From his position perched on a stool in the corner Johnny could now make out people heading towards the meeting room at the back. Up by the bar his father was taking orders and trays laden with drinks were being passed across. The gentlemen of distinction were making their way over and were soon to be gone from Johnny's sight altogether. As the chatter eased the door slowly closed behind them. He was now left alone in the company of just the fishermen and a younger couple who despite not being on the invited guest list, were at least finding their own entertainment entwined in the corner.

It was time for bed. Still puzzled by the evening's activities he climbed the stairs and headed for his room. He had many questions but he would have to wait until morning now to assuage his curiosity.

Behind the closed door his father had put aside the small room for the sole and private use of his invited guests. Only seven were present in all but these were the select few. Their names included: Dowie, Tweedie, Maitland, Houston, two by the name of Robertson and finally Walker. The subject was golf and they had been selected by Mr. Dowie to consider the proposal of forming a new club to be called The Liverpool Golf Club. By the end of the meeting the proposal was carried and a club was formed that would prove to be one of the most influential and significant golf clubs in the history of the game. John Ball, Johnny's father, would provide rooms at The Royal Hotel. In effect it would act as its first clubhouse. The date of 15th May 1869 would be etched into the annals of golfing history. No one knew it at the time but the small village of Hoylake would soon be transformed for ever as would the life of that little boy who had crept down the stairs and whose curiosity had got the better of him.

~

Johnny appeared much later than normal for breakfast the following morning. Last night's activities had left his head swirling with sounds and scenes that had played out in his mind long after his head hit the pillow. It was his mother who finally woke him and roused him from his bed. She was a loving, if tough mother. Like all the children in the household, Johnny had duties to perform but maybe this morning she would be a touch lenient.

'Late night was it Johnny?' she called out to him as he entered the kitchen somewhat bleary-eyed.

'No mother. I just couldn't sleep', came the reply. It was accompanied by a brief questioning glance in her direction.

'Oh, I just wondered. Thought I might have noticed a young lad skulking round the bar last night, but I could have been wrong of course.'

Johnny quickly averted his gaze and moved over to the stove. His porridge was just about ready.

It didn't take long for Johnny to obtain the full story behind last night's events. After some probing, his father was more than happy to explain. Luckily he had had no idea that his son had been in attendance watching events as the guests arrived. Had he known, Johnny's daily duties would most likely have been doubled. He would be grateful for his mother's tender silence.

Within days two more notable gentlemen arrived to stay at the hotel. Messrs Robert Chambers and George Morris were now out on the sandy wastelands of the warren opposite, sculpting a primitive but challenging nine hole golf course. George Morris was a popular gentleman in his home town of St. Andrews, but more significantly he was the elder brother of one of the greats of the game, Tom Morris. Tom was known by all within golfing circles as Old Tom and was a formidable character and influential man. A tall, solid, bearded man, he was a fine golfer and keeper of the greens at St. Andrews. As one whose vigour belied his 48 years of age he knew all that there was to know about this Royal and Ancient game. Having a knowledgeable and well-connected man such as George as their golf architect would prove extremely valuable to the newly established club. The virtues of The Liverpool Golf Club could now be promoted to its distinct advantage and to those who mattered in Scottish golf.

At the club's inaugural meeting a committee was formed at which Mr. James Muir Dowie was appointed the first captain. The well-spoken Mr. John Dunn was also elected to the committee and a treasurer and secretary were duly chosen.

Over the weeks that followed, the warren saw significant activity. It brought the arrival of small teams of men scattered across every part of the wasteland, some marking out holes, others in pairs, filling in the worst of the abundant rabbit holes. Johnny was fascinated by it all. He had a perfect view of the proceedings from his front bedroom window. This land had been Johnny's playground. Now he was intrigued and mystified by all that was happening. What were they doing with all their rods and sticks and why were they filling in some of the smaller rabbit scrapes yet making others even bigger?

'Please sir. May I ask what you are doing?' Johnny enquired.

'Building a golf course young man,' Mr. Chambers replied. These here will be the bunkers or hazards that the players will need to avoid when they come to play over the new links.'

Mr Chambers took several paces to the left and pointed to a flatter area of short finely-cropped grass.

'And these will be the greens. The rabbits are the ones who will do the work for us here, keeping the grass short and tight.' Together they wandered over the lush, springy turf.

'And where that feather's been placed, we'll cut a hole, and also over there.' He pointed further to his right.

Johnny stared on in open-mouthed amazement, his imagination running away with him.

'Can I play?' he blurted out.

'One day young man, if you show the talent and the desire....'

'Can I help you make the holes then and put the feathers in the ground?'

On evenings after school Johnny went out to help at every opportunity. Messrs Morris and Chambers were content for him to do so for they were also astute enough to know that it did no harm to please the son of their clubhouse owner back at the hotel. Hard work was nothing new to Johnny. He would regularly spend weekends helping to herd the cattle and cut the hay on his grandfather's farm, only a mile or so away in Great Meols. There was a tough, determined spirit in this young lad, one that would stand him in good stead for the challenges ahead.

Saturday 5th June 1869 saw the first formal meeting of The Liverpool Golf Club and a lively meeting it was at that. Again Johnny's father provided drinks at discounted prices which pleased everyone present. Business over, Mr. Morris and Mr. Chambers, the latter a formidable amateur golfer in his own right, played a demonstration match round the newly established links. However theirs wouldn't be the only entertainment on display that day.

For over twenty years now this wide expanse of predominantly flat land stretching a full mile and a half south towards the village of West Kirby, had not just been home to the rabbits, kestrels and skylarks. It was also one of the key horse racing venues for The Liverpool Hunt Club and a regular scene of colourful entertainment for one and all. Indeed such was the commitment of those who raced their steeds over the warren, that they had built their own two-tier wooden stand which provided basic but adequate accommodation for the day's racegoers. On warm summer evenings people from miles around would turn up in their droves transforming the warren into a lively scene. Hooves thundered to the cheers of punters who placed their hard-earned brass on the outcome of races. Over the general chitter chatter the sounds of bookies could be heard shouting out odds to anyone who was interested. All around the bright colours of jockeys' silks turned heads and the warm, sweet smells of horses filled the senses. Today though, strangely clad gentleman in knickerbockers and tweeds carrying golfing sticks vied for the attention of the massing crowds. On this occasion they occupied the terrain to the left of the wooden racing rails but that wouldn't always be the case in the future.

Normally Johnny would be out watching the racing but today he was more interested in this strange game of golf. As he stood watching from the sidelines, hands thrust deep into his pockets, a magnificently holed chip shot from Mr. Chambers raised a joyful round of applause from the ladies watching. Johnny was suitably impressed. His face lit up with boyish glee.

Amongst the men and womenfolk one proud couple pushed their pram, in and out of the bustling crowd. Inside their five month old child was fast asleep. The going for the couple was uneven. Seeing the rutted path immediately in front of them, Elisabeth Hilton was forced to twist her pram sharply to the right. Johnny hadn't spotted it. Too eager to see the golfers finish off their last few shots, his head was elsewhere and in a frantic twist of arms and legs he tumbled to the floor. As a robust young lad, he wasn't hurt but he was certainly embarrassed. With a swift dust down and a rub of the knees he sprang to his feet and was suitably quick to make his heartfelt apologies to the couple and child.

'I'm so sorry. Is he alright?' Johnny enquired as he looked into the pram.

The baby had been woken but there was no harm done. However for a moment as the young child's eyes met Johnny's the two exchanged broad smiles.

'Don't worry. He's fine,' Mrs. Hilton replied. Satisfied by their reassurances, Johnny doffed his cap, bid them good day and was gone.

The meeting between the sprightly seven year old and the young child was a brief one. However little did anyone know at the time but the paths of John Ball and the five month old Harold Horsfall Hilton would cross in far more significant ways over the years to come.

Within a month George Morris had brought his son Jack down with him from Scotland. Initially it was to help out on the links. However after a few weeks George suggested that it would be in Jack's best interest to return to Scotland. Jack disagreed and decided to hang on to try things out for a further week at least. He remained, was appointed the club's professional, and would live out the rest of his working life here at Hoylake. He was to form part of the very life blood of the club.

Back at the hotel not only was Johnny's father growing to like his golf, but as landlord he also saw the financial advantages of providing good quality clubhouse facilities for the club's members. Ever the keen businessman his offer to rent out one of his rooms for £3 a year was accepted and wooden lockers or boxes were built to enable members to store their clubs. For the time being they would have to be stored on the floor before money for a carpenter could be raised to fix them to the walls. By August Jack Morris, the newly appointed professional, was also happily set up in an old horse box at the back of the hotel and was content putting his crafting expertise to good use through making clubs during the week and giving lessons at the weekend to the now rapidly growing number of members.

It was on one wet and miserable Saturday, that a bored Johnny Ball decided to go exploring. With a gale blowing in from the west his help would not be needed on his grandfather's farm and there seemed to be far more of interest to him, in checking out the contents of his father's hotel. He pushed open the door of one of the rooms. Inside he was taken by the myriad of well-crafted boxes laid out on the floor. The strong smell of linseed oil was unmistakable. Finding one such box or locker partially ajar, he gingerly opened the lid and peered inside. For a moment he knelt motionless, his eyes transfixed by the contents inside. He started counting – one, two, three….at least seven immaculately crafted wooden golf clubs. With great care he bent over, picked one up and laid it across his hands. The balance seemed perfect. He stood up and posed as if to swing.

At that precise moment, a handle turned in the door at the far end of the room and the imposing figure of his father entered.

'What the hell do you think you are doing?' he bellowed.

'Just looking,' came the frightened reply.

'More than looking I think. You've no right to be in here. Put that back immediately. Gentlemen pay good money to store their valuable clubs here.'

In an instant Johnny laid the club back down in the box, closed the lid and shot out through the back door. His father tried his best to follow but soon realised the chase was pointless. He quit his losses and walked back out onto the lawn that sloped down to the sea. There were few customers in as yet and he wasn't needed at the bar for the time being, so he took his time before coming back. If truth be known, he was seething. He needed time to cool down and he knew the perfect man to let off steam to. John knocked on the door of the old horse box, and pushed it open.

'Morning Jack,' he bellowed out.

'Morning John,' came the reply

'Just caught my son messing about with someone's clubs in the locker room. Could have done untold damage.'

Jack's face winced in acknowledgement of his displeasure and then in his quiet Scottish lilt he ventured a reply.

'I'm not surprised one wee bit John to be honest. I've been watching him for days now. He's itching to play. With all that's been happening round here of late, in truth it's only to be expected. Don't be too hard on him. Leave it with me. I'll have a wee word.'

'Hmm, maybe you're right, but I'm not having my son interfering with other people's property. He'll be the death of me,' John replied, and with a very nimble movement for a man in his fifties, turned on the spot and marched out.

It wasn't until the following day that Jack caught Johnny's eye as he ran past the back of the hotel.

'Hey there young man,' he cried out. 'I've got something for you.'

Johnny came swiftly to a halt and followed Jack back into his hut. Jack strolled over to his counter, reached underneath and brought out a little gift.

'I believe you were searching for something the other day. Well, maybe this is what you were looking for?' and with these words he presented Johnny with the most perfectly crafted golf club you might ever expect to see. What's more it was just his size.

'Would this be of any use to you?' Johnny was utterly speechless.

'Oh thank you Mr. Morris, Thank you, thank you,' Johnny enthused, skipping away in joyous excitement.

Within no time he was outside on the lawn swinging the club to his heart's content. In fact he just couldn't stop. For the next five minutes he was a human Catherine wheel. Behind him Jack stood in the doorway, looked on and smiled.

'Hey Johnny,' he cried out. 'Aren't you forgetting something?'

'What's that?' Johnny called back.

'Well don't you want something to hit?' He replied.

'Oh yes.'

As Johnny jogged back over to the hut, Jack retreated once more behind his desk and pulled out a small, hard, white sphere and placed it in Johnny's outstretched hand.

'Now don't lose it,' he cried out. 'It's the only one you're getting!' In an instant Johnny was gone and for the next hour, the lawn became a scene of flying turf and whirling arms.

These were to prove Johnny Ball's first essays at the game of golf, a game that would soon become his life.[1]

From the back kitchen window a hand pulled the curtains to one side. Johnny's mother had been distracted by the noise outside and as all mothers do, she wanted to know what was going on. The scene she saw warmed her heart. Johnny was hitting his golf ball back and forth on the wasteland opposite. She had never seen her son so happy. At times her husband would wield him the big stick but Johnny also needed encouraging. He needed the chance to be himself, to be free and to enjoy the innocence of youth. Things were changing rapidly at The Royal. Golf was drawing more and more people to the hotel. Perhaps there was a future for her son in this strange game, she thought.

For the next few weeks nothing could keep Johnny away from the warren. His father wouldn't let him practice on the newly established course but there was still plenty of free, flat ground that he could use where he wouldn't be disturbing anyone. From his school in the hamlet of Hoose in the centre of Hoylake Johnny would walk back home along the beach, enter the hotel through the back door, pick

---

[1] Bernard Darwin writes in John Brownbill's book 'West Kirby and Hilbre' of how Jack made 'a little club for master John Ball.'

up his club and ball and head straight off onto the warren opposite. As he ducked under the fence, the rabbits would scatter and for the next few hours the warren would be his all-consuming playground.

One evening the tall, bearded figure of his father came to join him. Under his arm he carried his gun. For years his wife Margaret had laid on sumptuous food for the guests at the hotel. More often than not it would be fish on the menu if the catches were adequate, but if her husband was a good shot, rabbit pie would be served up as well. It was a firm favourite. What's more it was free. Add in a few vegetables grown from their own family farm down the road and the couple could make good profits when the punters turned up hungry.

Her husband was on the prowl for fair game this evening and Johnny watched as his father picked off the rabbits one by one. Having been successful with his first three shots, John passed the gun over to his son.

'Here, you have a go son,' his father called out.

In truth the gun was far too big and powerful for a lad of his stature. Once the trigger was pulled, Johnny winced in pain as he reeled back unexpectedly from its violent kick.

A little shaken Johnny passed the gun back to his father who was now doubled up laughing. The rabbits were at no risk from that volley.

'Perhaps we'll have a go when you're a bit older,' he smirked.

Feeling belittled by his father, Johnny was none too pleased. In a fit of temper he picked up his club, swung it back and proceeded to strike his ball in such a way that it simply sailed off far into the distance. He had hit it almost as far as one of his father's best shots. In an instant it wiped the smile from his father's face.

'Hey that was good. That was very good,' he acknowledged.

'Go and pick that up and have another go.'

Now feeling a little bit taller Johnny sprinted over, picked up his ball and jogged back.

Once more he took aim and drove through the ball, but this time taking much more care. Again it sailed off into the distance, straight and true but this time even further.

'Pretty damn good.' His father declared.

'We could make a fair golfer out of you yet son.'

It was the first compliment John Ball Senior had ever paid his son. Throughout his young, brief life Johnny had received nothing but criticism from his father and he had yet to be hardened by it all. He wasn't used to such praise and his head swelled with pride. Again he ran off, retrieved his ball and arm in arm, both of them satisfied with their endeavours - father with his rabbits, Johnny with his golf shots, they made their way back to the hotel.

It wasn't long before his father put his head round Jack Morris' door again.

'You know Jack. My lad's got real potential,'

'That's certainly true Mr. Ball. I've noticed it myself as well. He's got a keen eye for a ball that's for sure. I'll look out for him, don't you worry Mr. Ball. He's a good lad indeed.'

The two gentlemen were clearly on the same wavelength but neither had time to squander. Johnny's father had a busy hotel to run and Jack, clubs to make. As the two bade each other good day it was clear that the future of The Royal Hotel and of golf at Hoylake was in good hands.

# The Grand Tournament

Johnny's world revolved around just four things: school, his home at The Royal Hotel, spending time on his grandfather's farm and golf. Beyond that he had no appreciation of the world outside Hoylake. Although the city of Liverpool was but an hour's journey time away, it meant nothing to him. However it was all coming closer. People were arriving from far afield. Life at the hotel was getting much busier.

His sisters were now old enough to clean and prepare the rooms and Johnny would help by collecting glasses and clearing the fire grates in the main rooms downstairs. Each had their duties and knew their place. All had to earn their keep despite their young age. It would be excellent training for their years ahead. As for the visitors to the hotel, they came with new attire, unusual accents and a different outlook on life. Many would stay on a regular basis. Golf would be their main pastime but partaking of the fresh sea air was also a major attraction. The hotel and the club were on the up. Likewise so was Johnny. With the long summer evenings he was now out on the warren as often as he could. His game was progressing well.

In the summer of 1871 the club was honoured to receive the patronage of Prince Arthur Duke of Connaught. From now on it was to be called The Royal Liverpool Golf Club, a name which would add even greater prestige to a rapidly expanding club. Befitting of its status it had also been enlarged to a full 18 holes. Many of these were now reckoned to be some of the toughest holes in Britain.

It was one day the following spring as Johnny was out on the warren that his eyes were drawn to a number of carriages coming down his road. As he looked up he heard a cry from the hotel entrance. It was that of an all too familiar voice.

'Johnny, here lad, quick, we need your help,' his father shouted over.

Johnny picked up his ball and club, ran back towards the hotel and with a nifty hurdle over the boundary fence, was there in an instant.

'Johnny, take these gentlemen's luggage up to rooms five and six,' his father called out.

'Yes father,' came his instant reply, as he slung the two bags over his shoulder.

Young Tom Morris was a man of no more than 20 or 21 years of age. He was accompanied by his father, Old Tom. As Johnny led the way up the stairs he couldn't help but overhear their conversation.

'Looks a braw course, like ye told me father, 'n' the breeze, weel that'll make it tough fur sure.'

'Bound tae be a braw one son. Your uncle bult` it,' came the reply.

Johnny was confused by this strange language and their foreign accents. He could work out some of what they were saying but he was becoming more and more intrigued by these two gentlemen.

He opened the door. Young Tom was getting the best room in the hotel. From its position high up it offered excellent views over the warren and out over the course.

The two were here to take part in a major competition in two days' time.

'Ah there she is,' Old Tom pointed out.

'N' th' hills ower there?' He looked over to Johnny for a response.

'Those, over west sir? They're the hills of Wales with the Dee Estuary in the foreground.'

'A braw scene indeed, a braw steid fur golf that's fur sure.'

Johnny looked mystified by these final comments. Until now he had found a way of being able to interpret their words but this time he was lost. Instead he just nodded in appreciation. It seemed the safest thing to do.

The two were eager to move on and the older of the two gentlemen was keen to be shown to his room.

'If you'd like to follow me sir,' Johnny interjected.

As Johnny led the way into the adjoining room, Young Tom followed on to check he wasn't missing out.

No expense had been spared for these two gentlemen. Old Tom was to have a similarly sumptuous room next door.

'I've left your luggage here sir,' Johnny remarked. 'Is there anything else I can do for either of you?'

'Not at all, young laddie. Thank you for your trouble,' came Young Tom's reply as he held out his hand, placing a penny in Johnny's palm.

'Well thank you sir,' Johnny replied still looking a touch confused by their strange utterances.

Johnny turned to leave but just as he did so, the younger gentleman called back to him. His words stopped Johnny in his tracks.

'Wait there a minute, before you go. Let me see that dancin you have there,' he remarked.

Johnny stared back at him. He had no idea what he was saying.

'Ye dancin, yer club.'

Johnny twigged and handed over the small but well-crafted golf club he was carrying. Jack had long since made him a newer and bigger one but it still bore the hallmarks of his skilled workmanship.

'That's a fine club you have there, but do you know how to use it young man?'

'Oh yes sir I practice with it every day on the warren, out there sir.'

'Go on then, show me what you can do,' came Old Tom's reply and ushered him out of the door.

In an instance Johnny had made his way back down the stairs, out across the road, under the fence and onto the warren. He was closely followed by the two gentlemen. They exchanged a few words on the way.

'He's got his father's spirit, that's fur sure,' Old Tom muttered to his son.

The commotion of footsteps back down the stairs had drawn the attention of a few others including his father and as Johnny prepared to play his shot, he now had quite an audience. Johnny drew back the club but his strike was quicker and jerkier than normal and the ball veered off to the right.

'Here, have another go, a bit slower this time.' Young Tom called out as he took one of his own balls out of his pocket and threw it over to Johnny.

He was right. Johnny had snatched at that one, but he wouldn't make the same mistake the second time around. This time his swing was much slower, more rhythmical and more fluid. The result was as near to perfection as he could make it for a lad of his slight stature. It was Young Tom who led the applause and it was quietly but enthusiastically followed by all who were present.

'Stoatin shot,' Young Tom called out.

Johnny turned to the group, smiled, and raced off to retrieve the balls. The watching party retreated and headed back into the hotel.

'You're right,' Young Tom remarked to Johnny's father. 'He's certainly got something about him.'

'Maybe so,' Mr Ball replied, 'We'll see. I must apologise for my son's behaviour. It's not the way we would normally greet our guests. Can I instead gentlemen, welcome you formally to The Royal Hotel.'

'Thank you. No need to apologise though John,' Tom replied. 'The lad needs encouraging in the craft of the game.'

'He's still young but we certainly can't keep him off the warren. He's out there day and night. But to more important things... what time would you like to eat tonight gentlemen?' he enquired.

'Seven o'clock will be braw, John.'

'I'll reserve a table for you over by the window,' John confirmed.

And with that the two gentlemen retired to their rooms.

When they came down to dinner later, the first thing that was placed on the table in front of them was a golf ball.

'I insisted he gave it to you back Mr. Morris.' John uttered.

'Not at all', Young Tom replied. 'Let him keep it, he can practice with it.'

'That's very generous of you sir,' John replied. 'He'll be thrilled.'

'Now what can I get you gentlemen?'

Johnny was up extra early the following morning. It was the Saturday of the Spring Meeting and he had a competition to play in, as did many of the club's members. His tee time in the boy's competition was early - 9.10 am and his father was waiting for him with a hearty breakfast. Normally, Johnny would make his own, but this morning, he was being spoilt. It was a special day.

'You're a lucky lad my son,' his father remarked as he greeted him.

'Someone here's left you a present.' He placed the golf ball on the table.

Johnny's eyes lit up. 'Really, that's for me?' Johnny shrieked.

'Yes and do you know who those gentleman are who have left it for you?' his father responded.

'No,' came the reply.

'They are the two greatest golfers in the world today. The one with the beard is Jack's uncle – Old Tom Morris. He's the keeper of the greens at St. Andrews. He's won the Open Championship, the greatest championship in the land, four times already. The other gentleman is Young Tom, his son. He's now won it three times in a row. He's so good they've let him keep the Championship Belt. They're the best in the land. Some say the best that's ever lived, son.

28

Praise from those two is praise indeed. Talk to Jack, he'll tell you. They'll be playing in the competition over the next few days. You won't get better than them. Make sure you watch them in the competition tomorrow. Now eat your breakfast.'

Johnny's father was a strong disciplinarian and Johnny had never disobeyed him before for fear of enticing his wrath, but there was also a gentler side to him as well. On this occasion he was proud of his young son and how he had performed in front of the two most influential men in the world of golf.

Johnny tucked into his food as if it was his last meal. He was out in just an hour's time. He would be competing in the boys' competition this morning and he would be grateful for all the sustenance he could get.

In anticipation of his playing in the boys' championship Jack had made Johnny a full set of clubs (only five in total but these would be all he needed). It included a putter, two spoons[2], a cleek[3], and a newly developed club - a lofting iron[4], a club which Johnny was beginning to truly master.

He was hoping he would be master of his game full stop this morning.

---

[2] In the early days golf clubs were not numbered according to their degree of loft as they are now. They were given names. A spoon was the modern day equivalent to a higher lofted wood, possibly a 3 wood.

[3] A cleek is the equivalent to a 3 iron, a club with relatively little loft and thus one that is generally used for gaining distance.

[4] A lofting iron as its name suggested was used to impart loft to the ball to help clear obstacles in front of the golfer. As Johnny became more experienced his superior technique enabled him to be able to improvise and use a steeper faced club to achieve the same result.

As Johnny set off for the first tee there were more than a few who were keeping their fingers crossed for him. Poking their faces up against the corner of one of the upper floor windows, were five young girls - his sisters. Elisabeth and Margaret were the two oldest at fourteen and thirteen respectively. Katherine, aged eleven came next. In the background was Annie, ten and finally there was Ada, a lively and pretty young nine year old. More eager than all the others combined, Ada enthusiastically pushed her sisters aside in a desperate battle to catch a view of her talented brother through the grubby window. All four were wishing Johnny well more than anyone else this morning. It was a big day for him.

'Come on Johnny,' they shrieked as they watched him stride out with his small complement of clubs slung under his arm. As they called out so they turned to each other and giggled in excitement as only young girls do. They were his biggest supporters and were as proud as punch of their little brother.

Things were going well for Johnny in the early part of his round. However an almighty hook with his second shot to the 12th green sent his ball careering over a high mound and into the wild grasses beyond. It was nowhere to be seen. He would have to drop another with a one stroke penalty, but he only had one ball left. It was the one Young Tom had given him. Must he really use it? It meant everything to him. He would be heartbroken if he lost it, but he had no choice. It was do, or die. An hour later he had sunk a three foot putt at the last and had sneaked home with a five. He would need to wait for others to finish before discovering whether his score would be good enough, but he felt confident of his chances. His father was there at the finish too, as were Jack and the Morrises. Cruelly the young girls had been ordered to stay inside. Johnny had been taking part in activities which were well beyond the comprehension of four young girls, or so their parents thought. However there was one player who did see Johnny finish and he wasn't too bad a player himself.

'Weel played Johnny,' Young Tom called out.

Johnny looked over and smiled but as he did so he pointed to his ball.

Young Tom knew what the gesture meant and returned his smile in equal measure.

It took a good hour or so for all the contestants to finish but in the end Johnny's score was good enough to take the top prize.

Winning that medal was a major achievement for Johnny. What's more it had been extra special to have succeeded with the ball that Young Tom had given him and with the eyes of the very best watching from the side-lines. The following day he would be out watching Young Tom and the other professionals for himself.

The girls may have been barred from coming out to watch Johnny's final few putts but no-one was going to prevent them from celebrating their brother's grand victory. The party took place, with his mother's permission, in his bedroom just before he went to sleep. She had helped the girls to bake a celebration cake and it was scoffed, crumbs and all long before morning came. A few slices were meant to have been saved for their father, but greedily these were eaten under the covers a few hours later, round about midnight!

The following day's events were taken far more seriously by all concerned. There were rich pickings to be had.

In order to mark the arrival onto the scene of the newly established Royal Liverpool Golf Club, the committee had sent out invitations to the most distinguished clubs throughout the land to compete in this, the club's inaugural professional event. A massive figure of one hundred and three pounds, fifteen shillings had been raised from members. Of this sum, fifty five pounds was to be used as prizes and a further eight pounds to be spent on cutting a fine silver medal for the victor. This left more than forty pounds to be divided amongst the winners, twice the sum on offer at the Open Championship that year at Prestwick. As a result it was no surprise that all the top professionals had turned out for this two round competition. Most had come down from Scotland to take part but there were also representatives from the host club and clubs from further south such as Westward Ho, London Scottish and Royal Blackheath.

The main prizes were significant enough but these sums were easily matched by the side bets being laid on the eventual winner. This was common practice in most sports but had become the norm at St. Andrews. Side betting on horses and golf was a way of life for many. However whilst golf was relatively new to Hoylake, the practice of betting wasn't. The regular race meetings on the warren were responsible for that but now the arrival of the world's greatest golfers had provided a perfect excuse for significant money to be lost or won.

Johnny felt different when he woke this morning. There was an air of confidence, almost cockiness about him today.

After all, he had just shown himself to be the best young golfer in all of Cheshire. He also had a further interest. He now saw himself as best friends with the competition's firm favourite and the world's best player, Young Tom Morris.

Before coming down the hotel stairs he had taken great pride in pinning his winner's medal to his chest. Like any young lad he wanted the world to know he was the best around. In the entrance porch his mother was busy sweeping up the leaf litter that had built up at the hotel entrance.

'Hey, young man, what on earth have you got there?' She pointed to his chest. 'There's no way I'm letting you out there with that thing on display,' his mother called out. 'Who do you think you are that you can show off like that? Take that off right now. That's to keep at home, not to flaunt about. You don't do that. Them gentlemen out there, if they want to do that sort of thing, well that's fine. They are different to us, but we don't do that here. Hand it over right now.'

Johnny's mother was from strict Welsh working class stock. She wouldn't have her son behave in such a way. To conduct oneself with true modesty was what she expected of all her family.

Johnny was shocked. He unpinned his medal and handed it to his mother.

'You can have it back later but you keep it in your bedside drawer and it stays there,'

Johnny's demeanour instantly changed. From being the young self-assured, almost arrogant boy, he was now the young lad who had just been taught a lesson. It was one he would learn from and which he would take heed of for the rest of his life.

Out on the course the first round saw Davie Strath take the lead with an 82. Strath, a Scottish professional and previous Open winner from North Berwick was followed three shots back by Bob Andrews and Young Tom Morris. Other notable professionals such as Tom Dunn, the professional at the London Scottish club, and John Allan, another Scot, were both a further shot back. Sadly Old Tom's chances appeared to be gone. He had finished with a poor 92.

Throughout the day's proceedings Johnny was out on the course watching events like a hawk. He wasn't going to miss a single shot played by his new friend. Young Tom had started badly in the first round, taking an eight after finding a ditch at the 2nd but he was now making a comeback. Behind him Tom Dunn, one of his challengers wasn't faring nearly so well. Twice he had had the misfortune of hitting the wooden rails used for racing. His bad luck had ended his chances.

Meanwhile in the background, Johnny's hero was performing well. As Young Tom sunk his final putt at the 18th green Johnny punched the air with delight. His boyish glee was well founded. His score proved sufficient to clinch victory ahead of his fellow Scot, Davie Strath by a single shot. As Johnny's beaming face looked on he didn't fail to notice the smile and nod of the head directed his way from Young Tom. The large crowd was likewise thrilled to see the current three time Open winner prevail. It had been a good weekend all round. Also amongst the spectators was Johnny's father who was happily weighing up what this would mean in terms of his son's future, the Club's standing in the game and the financial prospects for The Royal Hotel.

# Tough Times

The growth of the game on the links was also having a positive impact on Hoylake as a whole as it was bringing with it an increasing demand for housing. Much of this was at the luxury end, driven by rich Liverpool merchants now wishing to live on the Wirral. At the same time they could also enjoy the benefits of being members of an esteemed new golf club. Over the next few years the construction of new houses would be encouraged by the coming of the railway from Birkenhead docks. The new railway was linked to a tramway connecting passengers to the Woodside ferry terminal for the short ride across to the now booming city of Liverpool. Johnny would often notice many familiar faces alighting from their carriages, the same ones he had seen in the hotel all ready to take the train onwards towards Birkenhead and Liverpool. He would take the trouble to wave them off from the station and he would receive their fond cheerios in return. Johnny now felt part of the scene in Hoylake. People recognised him. He was the cheery young lad with the golfing talent and with the energy to match, the one who greeted the guests with their strange accents as they arrived at the hotel. He was the one who bid them a fond farewell a few days later as they departed on their journeys home. Johnny was happier than he had ever been. He felt loved and valued. He was now an integral part of the life at the hotel and of a successful and growing club.

The Royal Liverpool Golf Club was by no means the only attraction in the town. The trains were also bringing in visitors keen to sample the coastal waters and to relax on the sands. In his earlier pre-school days Johnny would mess around almost alone on the beach at Hoylake. Now the company was many and varied as he and his friends made their ways home from school. Out at the water's edge the myriad of brightly coloured four-wheeled bathing machines were a common sight as they hid the modesty of their owners within. Above them higher up amongst the sands couples promenaded in the late evening sun oblivious to the boys playing in front of them. Hoylake was getting busier and there was money to be made through visitors and golf. Even schoolchildren were benefitting. It wasn't long before caddying work became available at the rate of 3d a round, efficiently marshalled by Jack from the back of his workshop. The spring and autumn meetings were the busiest, although there was also plenty of work for the regular caddies most Saturday mornings. Johnny wasn't one of them, though. He had a different focus. His mind was set on playing the game, not watching or helping.

Despite his popularity amongst members, as a junior, Johnny had no rights to play over the links unless accompanied by a full member. However this didn't stop him sneaking on at times at the far end of the course where he was out of sight of most of those who mattered. More often or not, he would practise on the rough ground well to the right of the green opposite the clubhouse. On occasions when the pressures in the hotel eased, Johnny's mother would nip out and linger by the fence and watch him practising. She would never let on to anyone, but of all her children it was Johnny for whom she held her deepest love. Her girls were strong. They had each other for company but Johnny was a lad on his own, a young fighter and he had yet to make his way into the world. As she peered over the fence, she wondered what the future might hold for him.

Johnny's success had not gone unnoticed in the club. He was steadily improving. The regular competition he was getting was beginning to toughen him up and to build a determined streak in him. There was no doubt that he had inherited many of these qualities from his father who had now become a fine golfer in his own right. As one who had never touched a club before, he had mastered the game well enough to have got down to scratch within just 18 months. In time the strong father – son partnership would become a match for anyone.

~

The year of 1872 proved to be the happiest of Johnny's early life. He had achieved success in his first major competition and it meant the world to him. There was now a new fresh sense of freedom coursing through his veins.

Sadly within months all this would change. In the back of his mind he knew that his mother wasn't her normal self. She had been rising far later in the mornings over the last few weeks and he had often heard her coughing violently during the day. The doctor had visited a number of times. Johnny was concerned.

His father had been up a good hour. Johnny himself had been awake since the wee small hours. He knocked on her door.

'Is that you Johnny?' She had recognised the weak tap on the solid oak door.

'Yes mother.'

'Come on in Johnny.'

Timidly, with head down, he shuffled over to the bed. When he finally looked up the sight that greeted him left him open-mouthed. His mother seemed a shadow of her normal self. Even in the faint candlelight, the white ashen colours of her face now matched those of the tired-looking bed sheets. It was all she could do to utter a few breathless words from between her dried out lips. As he spoke Johnny's head dropped. It was as if he couldn't bear to see this now wizened old woman, his mother, who lay before him.

'Have you had your breakfast yet Johnny?'

'Not hungry mother.'

'You need to eat Johnny. Keep your strength up.'

'Yes mother.'

'Are you going out golfing later?'

'Yes, mother.'

'Even more reason to get some food into you. Have you still got those clubs that Uncle Jack made you?'

'Yes mother.'

'Well you make sure you use them Johnny. I want you to listen to me now. Whatever happens to me, you must keep playing. You're good Johnny. You could be a very good golfer one day – one of the best, Johnny.'

He looked up with surprise. He was worried.

'What do you mean – if anything should happen to you?'

'Never you mind. Just you remember what I said. I want you to keep playing Johnny,' and with that she squeezed his hand tightly and kissed him on the cheek.

'Now go and have your breakfast and do your duties and help your father.'

Johnny took one final, sad look at his mother, left the room and nervously descended the stairs to the kitchen.

'Where the hell do you think you've been?' his father shouted out as he entered.

'Went in to see mother,' he replied.

'Don't you be disturbing her now. She doesn't need you worrying her at times like this.'

Johnny turned his back and set about his work. He had been on the receiving end of his father's booming voice too often and he knew when to retreat and do as he was told, but he now felt trapped, all alone in his sad thoughts. He didn't like what his mother had said.

That evening the doctor was summoned once again. By the following afternoon of 10th May 1873 Margaret Ball, Johnny's mother was dead.

To say that Johnny was devastated was an understatement. His sisters found it equally hard. At first Johnny refused to accept her passing. She was still there, just asleep, he would say to himself. In time his state of mind changed. Anger filled his head. He would shout and scream at his father and his sisters, and at Mollie, the new housekeeper who now assumed the role of temporary nanny to the children. The girls' reaction was quite different. They became quieter, more subdued and clung to one another for mutual comfort. Whilst Mollie took on more responsibility for the care of the children the girls themselves were asked to do more in the general upkeep of the hotel. They resisted at first, objecting to this new matriarchal figure with whom they had no natural bond. She could never replace the mother they had lost. For many months the children became argumentative and the tears were many and frequent. Over time though, they began to accept the need to help out more and more around the hotel. The extra work helped them take their minds off the loss they felt, but not completely. The nights were the hardest and the siblings would often come together in their bedrooms before lights out until disturbed sleep took them through to morning.

It was Johnny who found it hardest to accept his loss. One afternoon Jack spotted him, head slumped in his hands at the end of the lawn.

Slowly Jack approached him and laid his hand on his shoulder.

'You alright Johnny?' he whispered.

'Leave me alone,' Johnny snapped.

Jack stepped back and retreated to his workshop. No words could console his young friend for now but maybe something else would.

A minute later he returned but this time he carried a small gift. Over his arm lay a red golfing jacket. He took it over to Johnny and placed it silently at his feet.

The forlorn young lad sat motionless at first, not seeming to acknowledge what had been left there. Then, slowly, he bent down and picked it up.

Turning his head he looked back over to Jack.

'Is this for me?' he called out.

'Yes,' came the reply.

Johnny picked up the jacket and slowly rose to his feet. Stretching out first with one arm and then the other, he eased it onto his small frame. It was a little too big for him, after all it had been made for an older, larger man, but instinctively he pushed his hands into its pockets. In the left he found a cap. He straightened it out and carefully secured it onto his head. It was a snug fit. Next with his right hand he delved into the other pocket to reveal a small coin; a sixpence.

'Is this for me as well?' he asked.

'Yes it is,' came the reply.

His face lit up. He had rarely been given money before.

'Thank you Jack,' he called over.

'Hey now Johnny, you take care of that sixpence. There's a story behind that little coin, and the jacket.'

Johnny looked over to Jack with an inquisitive air.

'If you've a few minutes I'll tell you,' Jack continued.

Johnny just nodded and looked at him expectantly.

'Well many years ago when Old Tom was starting out as a professional he learnt his trade from the greatest player of the day – Allan Robertson. Allan often played for money. They say he never ever lost a money match as a single player. He taught Old Tom all he knew as a club and ball maker and they grew up playing as partners together in challenge matches. They were never beaten. They were a truly great partnership. I know because I occasionally caddied for them in the last few years before Allan passed away. Allan used to give me a sixpence for my trouble. One day – the year was 1843 I think, before I was born, Tom challenged Allan to a match. Tom won a jacket. When I first moved down to take up this job at the club Old Tom wanted me to have something of his to take with me. It was that jacket. It's a bit worn and it's a touch too big for you at the moment but it has a grand history, that's for sure. That jacket is yours now Johnny. I've put a sixpence in the pocket for good luck. It set me on my way when I was a youngster like you. Keep them safe along with the ball that Young Tom gave you. You have what it takes to be as good as both of them one day Johnny, that's if you want to be.'

Young Johnny Ball was overwhelmed. He looked down at the sixpence in the palm of his hand and his fingers crept out from under the cuffs to feel the cloth of the jacket. He stood there open-mouthed, his expression transfixed. All he could do was to utter the simple words: 'Thank you Jack, I'll do all that I can to keep them safe.'

Jack turned towards him and for the first time in two weeks he felt sure he detected the faintest trace of a smile easing across the young lad's face.

~

The road to recovery was a long and rocky one for Johnny. Luckily he found ways to distract his mind. At weekends he would walk across the fields to his grandfather's farm in Great Meols. Occasionally he would help out with the haymaking or other jobs that were needed on the farm. He loved the freedom and the hard work. For him it was both therapy and independence in equal measure. His biggest comfort though, came from his golf. He would be out there on the warren every second he could. On the bad days when he found things so difficult to accept he would thrash at the ball in frustration. On others he would be reassured when shots simply whizzed off the clubface far into the distance. Despite those ups and downs, he always sensed there was someone close by, nurturing him, encouraging him and guiding him in spirit. The loss of his mother went deep, but he knew she was there. Johnny's pillow would be wet with tears every night but somehow she was keeping him going. His mind went back to those last words she had said to him:

'You could be a very good golfer one day, one of the best.'

Really? He thought.

Out on the warren those words would ring in his ears day after day. As his play improved he would start to believe in them. There would also be one other who would have faith in him as well. More often than or not he would be leaning up against the porch at the hotel entrance, watching him, checking on his progress and willing him on through his thoughts and prayers. It would be his friend, Jack.

Some days were good but there were others when nothing could make up for the grief that Johnny felt. On occasions he could barely speak. It was on one such gloomy morning that he poked his nose out from the back of the hotel.

Outside the strong winds had abated and a still calm had returned to the long stretch of barren shoreline. It was one which bore the evidence of last night's high tide leaving stranded clumps of seaweed exposed amongst the small islands of tall marram grass. Normally this would have been a call for Johnny to go searching along the strand line. Dead crabs, sea urchins, razor shells and jelly fish were often amongst the prize discoveries to be found by a keen young lad on such mornings, but not today. He had lost all interest in any boyish games. A quick look out across to the small fishing boats bobbing up and down and that was enough for him. He turned inland and headed over to see Jack in his workshop, housed in the old horsebox.

Jack's Aladdin's cave of wooden treasures was small but adequate for the time-being. Decorated with old straps of leather harnesses hanging from the many hooks, it still held the faint trace of sweet equine smells from its previous existence. Today new life was being breathed into the space that once housed the high spirits of horses, jockeys and their highly diligent grooms. Now a large, sturdy workbench took up much of the room to the rear and to the left and right, wooden shafts of semi prepared golf clubs lined the side walls. Wood chippings, the remnants of skilfully crafted golf club heads were scattered on the floor and in the corner blocks of gutta percha, resin from Malay tree sap, decorated the artisanal scene. These were soon to be fashioned into newly formed golf balls courtesy of a custom-made iron clamp that would mould the balls into shape. All around was evidence of Jack's prowess as a club maker. His workshop had become the engine room that would help drive the club forward and produce the golf clubs that the members demanded in quantities that Jack could now barely supply. He was hard at work as Johnny entered.

'How are you Johnny?'

Johnny's long face needed no qualifying and Jack picked up on his mood immediately. He needed to be put to work.

'Fancy a new driver?'

'What, for me?' Johnny replied.

'Certainly, but you'll have to make it.'

For the next four hours Johnny was gripped by everything Jack taught him and by the end, a wooden block, which in Johnny's eyes had at first been more suited to firewood, had taken on the shape of a well-crafted head of a new wooden driver. He would return again tomorrow to finish off the work he had started.

Back in the hotel Johnny's father had thrown himself into his landlord duties as his means of coping with his grief. It took his mind off things but he also had a business to run. Away from the hotel he too would focus on his golf and he played most weekends when time allowed.

His son was still at school but he hadn't many years left to go now. Johnny never talked about his mini golf successes amongst his school friends but it was well known that he was the young golf star whose father ran the hotel up the road. Youngsters by the name of Farrar, Cook, and Tweedie, the latter being the son of the club's Secretary were all showing promise but Johnny was the one who really stood out. As a result small challenges would often be thrown up by his class mates. All were trying to get him to show off his golfing talents. Johnny was normally reluctant to rise to the bait and generally ignored these taunts whenever they came his way. In any case, he was in no state of mind to take them on. However, after school one afternoon he finally relented.

One young lad had begged and begged him to show how far he could hit a ball along Hoylake beach. Johnny's feelings of anger and frustration had risen to fever pitch and he needed to let off steam. In an instance he dropped a ball on the ground and in a wild maelstrom of flying sand and mud, his strike sent it soaring off into the distance and out of sight. His admirer looked on in open mouthed amazement.

'Good shot Johnny,' the lad called out.

The person who spoke was a young six year old Harold Hilton, the very same young Harold who Johnny had disturbed in his pram years before. Little did Johnny know that the two of them had met before, nor would he know that this one shot would prove all the encouragement Harold needed for him to take up the game which would later become his life. Johnny had laid down a challenge to little Harold. It would prove to be the first of many.

Johnny returned three times to Jack's workshop over the next few weeks. The final crafting of his club would take longer than expected. There was the elegant shape of the head to be finished, a bone plate to be secured to its base and sanding and rubbing down to be completed. The head needed varnishing and waxing. The shaft had to be carefully inserted into the head and to be glued securely in place. The next stage saw the whipping being wound around the hosel and a fine leather grip being fitted with the full loving care and attention that all clubs need. Jack was providing a personalised service which the members truly valued. More importantly the skills that Jack was teaching were helping his young pupil to overcome the grief that he still felt. It was also instilling in him a touch and feel for club and ball that he would transfer to his game in the years to come.

Over the next few weeks Johnny was there almost every day. One afternoon, whilst finishing off his driver, he turned to Jack and posed him a question that was to prove harder to answer than any he had ever put to him.

'Hey Jack', he asked.

'Is it a good job being a professional golfer? Can you earn much money from it?'

'Well if you're asking me should you take it up for a living – well no, the answer's no. You might enjoy all that you're doing here young man but there's no money in it. You could do much better elsewhere Johnny. You're not the type of person to be earning a living from making clubs or by competing in tournaments for the rest of your life. Hey you're above all this anyway. There's more out there for you than this menial work.'

'But I love it,' Johnny replied.

'Working as a golf professional is no life for you young man. You will be looked down upon by all around. You'll be shown no respect out there. You can earn yours through playing the game as an amateur, through farming or taking over from your father in the hotel. You don't want to be doffing your cap to members when there's no money to be made. Don't bother getting into this game Johnny. In any case I wouldn't let you if you tried, nor would your father.'

'Wouldn't he?' Johnny wondered.

'He certainly wouldn't, believe me. Listen to me now. I know you're not on great terms with your father now, but keep your head down. There are worse jobs than working in a hotel, or farming. You could still be a successful golfer as an amateur. Trust me.'

Johnny needed time to mull this over. He had never been told what to do by Jack. Jack had always been the one to have taken the time to listen to him, to encourage him, not to tell him what to do or what not to do. This time however, a sterner message was coming through. Johnny was being left in no doubt that a life making clubs and balls was not the way forward.

Johnny wasn't convinced but maybe Jack was right. Certainly he loved helping out on the farm and if it didn't turn out to be profitable he could still work for his father in the hotel. Business was certainly going well there. He had some thinking to do.

Despite Jack's continuing encouragement and firm guidance, Johnny understandably achieved very little at the club over the next few years. His head was elsewhere. However he was getting stronger and his golf was improving. By the summer of 1875, at the age of just thirteen years old, he had managed to secure the Boy's Medal for the second time, sneaking home by one with a score of 98 for the seventeen holes played that day.

Further challenges lay ahead though. Christmas Eve had always been a special day for Johnny. It was his birthday. With Christmas to follow it was usually double celebrations for him! In the past you normally couldn't wipe the smile off his face for the presents he got, but with the loss of his mother, these last few years hadn't been the same. Maybe this year though, he was beginning to come to terms with things. Perhaps the passage of time had begun to ease the pain, be it just a little.

By 28th December everything changed. That morning he awoke to hear news that shook him to the core once again. Young Tom Morris, the twenty four year old champ, the idol he had followed when he came to Hoylake just three years previously, the gentleman who had given him his ball and those warm words of encouragement, had suddenly and unexpectedly died. It had happened on Christmas Day.

How could this be? Was he really to believe what he had just been told? Would he never have the chance to see Young Tom again, or to see him play once more? Johnny's mind and his emotions took him back again to that dark day two years ago when his mother passed away.

But he wasn't the only one to feel that loss. This time Jack also needed comforting. Young Tom was Jack's cousin. Not only had Young Tom been the greatest golfer in the world, he was also of his own flesh and blood. He had died so suddenly and in his prime. He had still so much to give to life and to golf.

Soon after Johnny heard the news he drifted into Jack's workshop. This time it was Jack who was lost for words.

'I'm sorry,' Johnny said and in that moment they hugged.

For the next few moments neither spoke. Eventually though, as Johnny turned to leave, he looked over to Jack and with a smile raised his hand. In it was a golf ball, but not just any old golf ball, and Jack recognised it as such. It was that special ball, the very same ball that Young Tom had given him all those years before.

'Ah, you've managed to keep hold of it then Johnny?' Jack replied in his light Scottish lilt.

'Well with it you've got his spirit there inside you as well. Take it with you all your life, Johnny. You could be as good as him one day,' he added.

'Thanks Jack,' came Johnny's reply, and slowly, very slowly he walked out into the morning sun.

~

No sooner had Johnny started to come to terms with his and Jack's loss, than unbelievably, tragedy struck yet again. The family had always doted on Ada, the youngest of the three girls. She was the sweetest one of them all but from birth she had always been the weakest. When disease hit the villages of West Wirral in the early spring of 1876 Ada struggled to find the strength to fight back. Hit by a heavy fever which quickly developed into full blown measles, she died in the evening of 13th May.

The whole household was paralysed by the loss. The grieving that took place within The Royal Hotel was distressing in the extreme. Even many of the hotel guests seemed to feel the pain and for a few days, time just stood still. The loss of a young child is hard for any family to take.

As the days passed it was only the mundane daily life of the hotel and the arrival of guests who needed tending to, that dragged the Ball family through this, the hardest of all times. Johnny took to the golf course and the girls once more sought comfort in each other's company. Johnny's father dug deep and with the help of the live-in nanny, who took on even greater responsibility for the support of the children, life somehow carried on.

# First Shot at the Open

It was Jack himself who would be the one to lighten the mood, and he would do so in the best way possible. In the summer of 1877 he married Johnny's cousin, Margaret. Johnny had never been especially close to his cousin as she had grown up in Llangollen, Wales, but now through their marriage, Jack had become part of the family. The bond which Jack and Johnny shared would from now on become ever stronger.

The good news off the course was being matched by that on the links itself. The reputation of the club was rapidly growing but the inevitable increase in membership was putting greater pressures on the warren. A piece of land which until recently had been an open, bare wasteland, ruled by the rabbits, foxes and by the occasional race-goer, was now being overtaken by the red-jacketed, moneyed golfers. These golfers were intent on building bunkers and greens wherever they wished. When players regularly found their shots cannoning off horse rails and golf balls coming to rest in large hoof marks, the men of influence were none too pleased. There was a growing band of passionate devotees to the game and racing was getting in the way. At the club's regular spring and autumn golf meetings the turn-out was impressive. The professional matches being arranged were attracting large crowds and significant local and national interest in golf at Hoylake. Conversely with the sport's increasing popularity, the racing lobby were suffering as were the local people who could no longer wander across what they thought to be, albeit incorrectly, common land. Locals, many of them fishermen, were seeing their freedoms restricted and the social camaraderie that came from mixing and betting on races was disappearing. Golf was a gentrified game often played by red coated socialites. It was alien to the Hoylake townsfolk and they didn't like it. Twice already this year members had reported the general public deliberately removing golf balls from play. Things came to a head one morning when a section of the 17th green was dug up and the turf found lying on the road in front of the hotel. Johnny's father was livid and immediately brought it to the attention of the committee.

A solution would have to be found and a meeting was held between members of the club and representatives of the local community. As ever the venue was The Royal Hotel. In the end the outcome would be a compromise. A very loose agreement was made whereby racing would cease, locals would refrain from their protests and in return for work on the course such as weeding, replacing of divots and the shaping of bunkers, they would be permitted to play on the links at allotted times. These privileges would be restricted to select numbers as determined by the club. A small number of brass discs would be issued to locals in recognition of this. In addition they would be able to supplement their incomes by carrying out caddying duties. At a time when fishermen were finding it more and more difficult to earn a good living from their trade this would prove to be welcome additional income. It would seem that all obstacles had now been cleared to ensure that golf would be the priority on the warren from now on. It would also allow Johnny the freedom to nurture the talent that he was so clearly showing.

Within a few months that talent was there for all to see. In no time Johnny had won the scratch medal at the club's main Spring meeting. He was still only fourteen. Soon plans were laid to play Mr. John Dunn, the holder of the club's gold medal. Johnny played him four times that summer and won on three occasions. Even the fourth match was tied. Johnny's confidence was certainly growing, but much was also down to his solid technique. From the moment he had watched his idol Young Tom win the grand match competition, he had decided to adopt his same grip. A flat palm grip with his right hand tucked underneath the shaft gave him the extra strength and the control he needed. It was an important step en route to perfecting the unique and refined swing he would use in future years.

~

There was little doubt that Johnny's father considered his son to have a special talent and his subsequent progress did nothing to dispel his belief in him. The time was nigh, he thought for a father to son chat.

It was still early and the mist was just beginning to clear from the Dee Estuary. As it lifted it revealed the distant silhouette of the Welsh hills. In the background the piping calls of the oystercatchers pierced the gloom and brought life to another day. A lone figure practised out on the 17th green opposite. From the open doors of the hotel a voice called out.

'Missed one yet?'

Johnny looked up and smiled. It was his father.

Slowly, he made his way over and not without a little discomfort, carefully bent over and picked out Johnny's golf ball from the hole.

'Jack and I have been thinking. How do you feel about having a go at competing in The Open at Prestwick in a few weeks' time son? I'd say you're ready for it. Jack could go up with you if you like. He could see his father and uncle but could be there to show you the ropes at the same time.'

Johnny had never thought this big before. He enjoyed his golf. He knew he was doing well but did he really think he could compete at the same level with all those professional cracks?

'I hadn't given it a thought to be honest, father', he hesitated in response.

'But yeah, I'd love to give it a try.'

'Well, that's good son,' his father replied. 'I'll leave you to talk it through with Jack then. He can sort out the details of getting there and entering. I can't come with you I'm afraid. I've got the hotel to run.'

There was nothing like competing in an upcoming Open Championship to focus the mind and Johnny was never going to be happy unless every part of his game was in 'A' grade condition. From now on there was barely an hour of the day when he was not on the links. But would his practice pay off?

The Claret Jug was to be competed for in September, in just three weeks' time. It was a relatively new trophy. The previous prize, the championship belt, was now in the possession of the Morris family after Young Tom, (sadly now passed away), had won it outright three times in succession between 1868 and 1870. Significantly, after Young Tom, Johnny would be the youngest competitor yet to compete in the Open. It was 1878 and he was just 16 years old.

The trip north to Scotland and to the Prestwick Links was an experience in itself for Johnny. Leaving early evening, the first leg took them by train from Hoylake through to Birkenhead Docks. From here they continued via horse-drawn tram to Woodside, followed by a choppy ferry ride over to Liverpool Exchange station. For one who had never set foot outside of the Wirral Johnny was transfixed by all that he saw. Despite the turbulent waters of the Mersey he insisted on staying out on deck as the ferry weaved its way in and out of the merchant vessels plying their trade into Liverpool. He was excited by the hustle and bustle of the docks and the lively comings and goings in a city lit up by gas lights that were just coming on in the early evening dusk. A light mist enveloped the quayside as the ferry pulled in, giving the dockside buildings an eerie atmospheric glow. Within half an hour they had boarded their train and were on their way north. From now on, the novelty of the journey began to fade and tiredness kicked in. The lack of any real comforts afforded by a basic, standard class ticket meant that any sleep Johnny got was fitful. In any case regular changes at Preston, Carlisle and finally Kilmarnock meant that by the end of the journey it was a case of survival rather than enjoyment or relaxation.

By the time the two arrived at 5 o'clock in the morning, over ten hours after setting off, Johnny was exhausted.

Tom, Jack's uncle, had pulled in favours from past acquaintances during his previous employ as keeper of the greens at Prestwick and had found them some basic, though comfortable lodgings half a mile from the course. Johnny spent the day catching up on sleep and building up his strength but on Jack's advice they took a stroll down to the links later that evening.

The terrain was more varied and hillier than he expected and the dunes and bunkers more pronounced. The links was comprised of just twelve holes rather than the usual eighteen. The format for the competition was also different - being three rounds each and just thirty six holes in total. Johnny would be glad of a good night's sleep tonight. He would need all his energies for his game tomorrow.

The following morning he awoke feeling refreshed and positive. He had a 9.30 am tee time and was out in just half an hour. Having secured himself a caddie, he walked over to the clubhouse. He needed to freshen up and change his shoes before heading out. He was about to step through the door when he was stopped by a well-dressed, burly gentleman who had blatantly stepped across his path to block his way.

'And where do you think you're going, mate?'

'Just going in to change my shoes, sir.'

'Not in here you're not. You think you're someone special then, do you, to come in here?'

Johnny was taken aback. There was no way this man was letting him in.

Johnny's caddie pulled him to one side.

'You can't go in there. Professionals can't enter the clubhouse, they're not allowed.'

Johnny did a double take. He was allowed to enter his clubhouse back home. What was the problem? He turned to his caddie for help.

'But I'm not a professional.'

'Maybe, but they don't know that. It'll cause a stink if you go in there. Them's the rules and you can't change them.'

The burly doorman hitched up his trousers and planted his feet firmly to the floor. Sure enough Johnny's caddie was right. The man had made his position perfectly clear. He had staked his spot. No one was getting past him.

This was a lesson to be learnt. Just as Jack had told him, professionals were treated as the lowest of the low. It took Johnny a few moments to take it all in, to understand all that had just happened but he had little time to spare. There was a game of golf to be played. He changed his shoes round the corner leaving his old scruffy pair in a nearby bush. Quickly he and his caddie weaved their way between the waiting players and over towards the tee. As they did so they passed many of the greats of the day. Mungo Park and his older brother Willie Park were both there. Also present was Jamie Anderson, and Tom Morris. All were previous Open winners. Johnny was in exuberant company. It was a competitive twenty six man field.

The good money was on Willie. As Johnny brushed past him a scruffily dressed gentleman tugged on his coat tails.

'I've got £2 on you Willie. I'm relying on you to show 'em what for,' he whispered in his ear.

He sneered back. He hated these chancers. He resented the fact that more money could be made from wagering on his prowess than he could ever make from playing the game himself. It wasn't easy making a living from golf.

The world of professional golf was new to Johnny. He was a young, naïve, fresh-faced debutant from Hoylake. This was a different world to the amateur game that he was used to, what with its brashness, the betting and the rawness of it all. It was a true eye-opener. Every golfer took great pride in their desire to beat their fellow man. This was serious stuff. Here livelihoods were at stake.

Johnny was paired with Ben Sayers in the first round. Sayers was a young Scottish professional from North Berwick who despite being five years older than Johnny was almost his equal in stature, at just 5 feet 3 inches. He had been a circus acrobat in his early years and had the muscles to prove it. They quickly struck up a bond. Here were two small rookies with fearless hearts, fighting the established experienced pros, both eager to make their mark.

Johnny started well and he was only three shots off the lead by the time he finished the first round. All in all he was quite content with his performance and he'd played well enough to be tied on the same score as many of the renowned golfers of the day, including Tom Morris, Willie Park, James Anderson and Bob Kirk. Up ahead, J.O.F. Morris led the field on a score of 50.

Johnny teed off for his second round with only a short break for lunch. In reality he needed longer to recover and build up his strength as a dismal eight early on immediately began to put doubts in his mind. It wasn't the best of starts.

In the background Jack followed, urging his young man on at every opportunity. In the first round all had gone smoothly but now things had changed. Now the seeds of doubt were beginning to creep in. Johnny was competing against top professionals out here. These were confident, bold individuals used to playing for big stakes with backers from their own clan who were cheering them on with every successful shot. As a young rookie from England, Johnny was alone and isolated with his thoughts. As he walked off the first green Jack could sense his head dropping. He walked over to his young prodigy and whispered in his ear.

'It's just one hole, it's gone, Johnny. I've heard the news up ahead. The leaders are blowing up. Concentrate, Johnny, concentrate.'

In truth Jack had no idea what was happening to the leaders, but his golfer didn't know that. It was clever psychology from the wise man, as from here on in Johnny's scores settled down.

The final round saw Anderson begin to command the stage. As a St. Andrean and the current holder of the Claret Jug he knew how to handle himself. He was more than used to these pressures. An incredible ace, (a hole in one), at the short hole got the crowds going. His golf from then on in never let up. Despite a brief challenge from Kirk towards the end, Anderson finally prevailed and the championship was his for the second time.

Johnny's score of 55 for the final round left him tied in fourth place with Bob Martin and eight shots behind the winner. Not a bad attempt in his first Open. Unlike medal competitions at home though, competitors who tied in the prize money were compelled to play off for their winnings the following day. Despite a good night's sleep Johnny's energies were nearly spent. In the end he wasn't used to four days of consecutive golf at this level of intensity. When the play-off took place the following day his game fell to pieces and he finished a full nine shots off the pace. It was still enough to earn him an impressive £1 in prize money, a tidy sum for a lad of sixteen. He had no intention of turning such money down and on Jack's advice, gladly accepted his well-deserved reward. It was a natural thing to do but his decision to accept the prize money would cause controversy in a few year's time.

Despite his play-off loss Johnny had played well in his first major championship. Remarkably another sixteen year old had likewise played well in the Open Championship only 9 years previously. He had also finished fourth. His name was Young Tom Morris. It was a fact that Jack was keen to point out to him later that evening.

By the time Johnny arrived back in Hoylake two days later the news of his fine showing had reached The Royal Hotel and his father was keen to lay on a small celebration for him. The members of The Royal Liverpool Golf Club certainly knew how to put on a party. Even his father's boss, Lord Stanley, had been told of his fine performance and had asked his gamekeepers to provide venison from his estate as the main course at the sumptuous dinner. Johnny's father provided the drinks and Mr James Muir Dowie brought the vintage claret. Even Johnny himself was in full voice that evening as later Mr. Thomas Owen Potter, dressed in his finery of dickie bow and breeches, conducted the singing with his ivory baton accompanied by Mr. 'Pendulum' Brown on the piano. The joyous evening went on into the small hours. Johnny's health was toasted many times over and the night was merry.

# Defining Times

There were rarely days at the club's spring or autumn meetings when the revelry and general high spirits between players could be topped. It was aided in no small measure by more than adequate facilities for socialising at the hotel both before and after matches. The hotel was the ideal venue. A large bar and lounge dominated by a roaring open fire where players could mingle and drink, provided the perfect opportunity to swap tales of rounds which improved with every drop of ale drunk. It also provided those with more adventurous personalities the chance to show off their sporting prowess in ways which surprised more than a few. Dividing the main bar area from the lounge was a tall, broad, open fireplace, one which served to heat both rooms. Being a good five foot in height it was possible to see through to the room opposite. After the drink had flowed and on the condition of a small wager, a player would dive through the flames of the fire and somersault into the opposite room, often appearing upright and nonchalant at the feet of customers engaged in genteel conversation next door. Once apologies had been made, the joker would then make the return journey, diving back through the flames to receive the promised sum from his backer in the room from whence he had come.

Such antics would on occasion be upstaged outside where on fine weather days players would goad each other into trying to clear the clubhouse with golf shots teed up from the long, sloping lawn behind the building. Success was eminently possible and could be more easily achieved when the wind came from a north westerly direction straight off the sea, thereby aiding the player with his play. The intention was not only to clear the clubhouse but also to land the ball as close as possible to the flag on the 17th green on the opposite side of the building. Needless to say, on many occasions disaster struck when the ball clattered squarely against the back wall of the clubhouse or worse still, smashed through the windows of the elegant building. When this happened, or indeed when Johnny's father caught such pranksters, severe words were exchanged and the culprits would be served a hefty bill.

In the same way that the club was going from strength to strength so was Johnny Ball and his ambitions were growing. He had just won his first pay cheque. It wasn't a fortune but it would certainly do. It had got him thinking. It wasn't that long ago that Young Tom had won considerably more than this. There was good money to be made from this game. Maybe, he thought, maybe the future for him was to become a professional. But was that touring life for him, mixing with those raw and outspoken characters, with their drinking and wagering? Sure, he was no saint himself, but it could be worth a shot. He thought back to those words of advice that Jack had given him. He did have other options as well. Those options weren't too bad: taking on the family farm, being able to work in his father's business at the hotel. He could still play his golf but maybe not as a professional as Jack had said.

He had made his decision. Jack was right. He would play the game as an amateur.

Back at the hotel his grandfather had moved in. The rigours of running a working farm were beginning to take their toll and he was keen for Johnny to become more involved with the running of the business. The old man had been living at The Green Lodge until now, a hotel which he owned just down the road but there was plenty of room in The Royal Hotel now and he missed the company of his family. His health was beginning to fail him and he was only too pleased to have his granddaughters around to fuss over him and take care of his needs. Johnny could update him on the farm in the evening and he was still able to walk down to The Green Lodge most days. He was a contented man in his old age and happy that The Royal Hotel had now become his home.

Johnny loved his golf but he also loved the outdoor life and in particular the challenge of managing a herd on a working farm. His grandfather had been genuinely pleased to see him take such an active interest in the farm. It had supported him for much of his working life. Now however, as Johnny moved into adulthood he needed to earn a living. He also yearned for that independence from his father.

Although his grandfather had employed a number of farm labourers it was always his intention that Johnny should take over the lease of the farm when he passed away. Johnny would still help out when required at busy times at the hotel but along with golf, farming would give him the sense of freedom and purpose he craved.

Johnny's experience of playing further afield at the Open had now given him the confidence to compete up and down the country. At the invitation of clubs such as Machrahanish in Scotland he would play against the top professionals in the area. All the time he could feel his game improving. Testing himself on new courses and against keen opposition was proving a perfect golfing education for him.

By the beginning of 1882 at the age of eighteen Johnny had finally earned his stripes at his home club. He was afforded membership of The Royal Liverpool Golf Club. It was to mark his turning of age at the club and by the following year he had become almost invincible as a player here. With his handicap now at plus six there was barely anyone who could match his play. That year he won The St. Andrews Gold Medal for the best scratch score on the day, The Dowie Cup for a similar feat at the Autumn Meeting and The Kennard Gold Medal for his success on the second day of the same meeting. For the next few years he would clean up in competitions, winning almost every scratch contest he entered. His home success had even been noted up in Scotland. The grandfather of golf, Old Tom Morris was to remark that, 'he was now the best amateur in the world,' - bold words indeed. Within weeks of Tom's comments Johnny's supporters had laid down an open challenge to any amateur to prove their worth against the rising young star.

This was tantamount to reawakening the old national rivalries between Scotland and England. Johnny may have been invincible at home but he had still yet to prove himself on the national stage. The Scots had invented the game and here was an Englishman whose supporters were seemingly suggesting that their man could out perform all from their homeland. It prompted an instant reaction. A contest would soon be arranged between the best that Scotland could muster and the young pretender from south of the border.

It was Douglas Rolland, a leading amateur and stonemason from Earlsferry, near St. Andrews, who would take up the offer. The match would be played out over thirty six holes on Rolland's home course at Elie, followed by a further thirty six at Hoylake. Rolland, a well-liked and affable man had gained a fine reputation for his long, straight hitting and it was indeed his magnificent driving that was to prove Johnny's downfall. His first head to head battle in the Kingdom of Fife proved a baptism of fire and a step too far for Johnny. Taunted at every missed putt by jeering partisan crowds he was on his own without Jack's support. He left Scotland seven holes down. He couldn't wait to return to home soil.

Whilst this was a large deficit to make up, Johnny nonetheless still had high hopes of turning things around. When Jack approached him practising out on the links before the return match, his concentration was so focussed on his game, that he barely noticed his presence beside the putting green.

'There's still time to change things around Johnny,' Jack called out to him. You know there are few who can beat you on your home course.'

'Thanks Jack but I'll sort it out,' Johnny's replied.

He sounded confident but there was a touch of irritation in his voice as well and Jack sensed it. His offers of technical advice had never been welcomed but at least he could still be there in the background, encouraging, supporting.

The following morning dawned fresh and bright but the same couldn't be said for Johnny's game. Not only was his putting poor, his driving retained none of the smoothness and rhythm that was his usual hallmark. Rounds of 90 and

91 put paid to any chances of a comeback and the match was lost. Even the following day when a further challenge of 36 holes was laid down, Johnny capitulated again from a winning margin of four holes up with five to play. It ended a period of utterly forgettable golf. There were many now who were seriously beginning to doubt whether he had the physical and mental strength to compete at this level.

~

It was the morning after his final match and the weather had turned from crisp and bright to dull and grey. Out on the River Dee, the haunting cries of the oystercatchers and the passing curlews pierced the gloom that had descended on the town of Hoylake.

Downstairs in the hotel Johnny's father was clearing away the remnants of the previous night's revelries. His pace was slower than normal, and his appearance more dishevelled. He was never a great fan of these early mornings. The smell of stale beer still lingered but he was used to this. Upturned glasses, broken bottles and fag ends were scattered in every direction. How was it, he thought, that it always seemed to fall on him to have to clear up all the mess? This morning it was especially bad. Over in the corner the fire was still smouldering and the thought of having to clean that out on top of everything else was almost the last straw. With a sigh he grabbed his bucket and trays and got to work.

Up in his bedroom Johnny slowly fastened the last buttons of his shirt and slipped on his battered old shoes. The sense of failure was still raw and he had little motivation for the day ahead. It was all he could do to stumble out of bed. His sole thought was to head for the fields, to the farm and some fresh air to clear his head. As he turned the stairs and his foot touched the final step, he was greeted by an almighty crash. In lowering his more than ample frame to the floor, his father had inadvertently clipped a stack of half full glasses to his right and sent them smashing to the floor. The effect was dramatic. The contents had sprayed his brand new sofa. Glass fragments were scattered everywhere.

'Damn it,' he bellowed.

He caught a fleeting glance of a figure moving in the corner. This wasn't the time for Johnny to have made an appearance.

'What the heck do you think you're staring at? Fetch a bloody cloth and dustpan quick, you useless piece of space.'

Johnny shot behind the bar and returned with the goods.

'Why the hell should I have to do this?' His father barked. 'Tell me what do you ever do in this damn hotel? This place will be left to you but you do nothing, nothing to earn it. Do you really want this place when I'm gone? I don't think so. You pay more attention to those farm animals round the corner than you ever do to this hotel, and to what end? Your grandfather did that all his life and he earnt virtually nothing from it. Why do you think he's still running The Green Lodge? Oh yes and you mess around on that bloody golf course as well and pretend you can play the game. You're no damn good at that either. How the hell did you lose to that guy yesterday? It was a pathetic performance.'

It was a full-on rant. Johnny had had enough. He didn't have to take this. He disappeared out of the door in a flash.

'Yes, go on. Leave it all to your father yet again. Go off to your cosy animals, why don't you?' his father called back.

The walk down to the farm was longer than normal this morning for Johnny, the going tougher in every sense. In anger and frustration he kicked out at the yellowish brown slush of sandy mud that had formed on the rough track after last night's rain. The mud sprayed the wooden picket fencing and splattered over his trousers. He grabbed a stick from the floor and smashed it on a nearby post sending debris in every direction. He picked up another and whirled it round his head before launching it with some venom into the bushes. By the time he got to the farm he was in no mood to turn his mind to the normal milking duties but he had no choice. There was no one else there this morning to help.

Stand Farm was normally a sanctuary for Johnny. It was his salvation - a space he could retreat to, where he could be himself. Away from golf he could recharge and throw himself into his work. Things had changed now. What was the point if there was no money in farming anyway? His father had laid his cards on the table. His grandfather was paying him a small wage to help run the farm but Johnny knew nothing about running it as a business, as a going concern.

The bitterness Johnny felt towards his father was still there. All these thoughts were running through his head. So father reckoned farming was worthless then, like his golf. Well great, and yet his grandfather had been a farmer all his life and never made any money from it then – can't be true, never, don't believe it. I'll show him. I'll prove it to him. I'll make him see there's money in farming. As for the golf, well damn the golf. I'm no good at that anyway, he thought.

It wasn't long before Jack got to hear of their disagreement back at the hotel. He was on the case straight away and within a couple of hours of the spat he poked his nose round the cowshed door. Johnny didn't see him at first. He was too engrossed in pulling udders. The teats were being tugged a little harder this morning and the cows didn't appreciate it!

'Hello Johnny', Jack called out.

Johnny looked up and was promptly anointed with a spray of white liquid.

He looked straight back down barely acknowledging the man standing behind him.

Jack moved closer.

'We need to talk',

'And why?'

'I've just been speaking to your father. He's not too happy.'

'Well you can tell him he's not the only one,' came the curt reply.

'He said you ran out on him when he needed help clearing up this morning.'

'Course I did. He reckons I'm no good at golf, and I could never make any money from farming.'

'Don't listen to him, Johnny. He's way off the mark. You're a damn good golfer and you could go places. You're the best player at the club by far. You know what Tom thinks of you and he knows his golf.'

'Yeah, but I should have slaughtered Rolland, and I lost. How pathetic is that.'

'It happens to us all,' Jack replied.

'I've done it. Your father's done it. We've all lost matches we should have won. All the great golfers have.'

'But how am I going to earn a living? I don't want to work in the hotel – not with him. And as for the farm, well it never made a profit. Grandfather never made any money out of it. That's what father said.'

'Well I don't know about that. Ask your grandfather. He'll tell you about the farm. He knows it like no other. Maybe if you really want to make it work, you can. He bought The Green Lodge only because he's growing too old for farming.'

'Maybe so,' Johnny replied. 'But it would be my life. If there's no money in it what's the point.'

'Speak to him Johnny.'

Johnny avoided his father for the next few days but he did at least make an effort to help out. He had the wisdom to know that it was in his best interest to at least make some kind of contribution in the hotel. His father was surprised one morning when he came downstairs to find every surface clear and spotless. A young cleaner had got there before him.

Johnny's grandfather spent most of his time down at The Green Lodge. It was easy for him to get to, and although he no longer served customers on a regular basis, he was still there most days to help run the business and sort out the usual staffing issues. Johnny would pass the hotel every day on foot as he set off for the farm. He decided to call in the following morning.

With slight trepidation he opened the door and stepped inside. Sure enough there was his grandfather sitting in the corner, engrossed in his newspaper, pint in hand. He spotted Johnny instantly and called him over.

'I thought you'd be down at the farm by now Johnny,' he called across.

'Yes, I should have been grandfather but I wanted to speak to you.' he replied.

'Of course. Grab a seat. What's the matter?'

With a heavy sigh, Johnny steeled himself and launched forth.

'The farm, grandfather, did you ever make any money from it? Father says you didn't.'

'Oh, does he now? Well he's wrong. Maybe he wants you working behind the bar at the hotel. True there isn't a fortune to be made in farming and it's always hard when you've got your rent to pay as well. Lord Stanley is a tough landlord. All the same I made enough running that farm. I've kept the lease going for you if you want it but I needed a more relaxing life. This place here is good enough for me now but farming's a young man's business. You need the stamina to make it work. You need to be up every morning. You know, you're doing it yourself every day. Don't you want it? Farming's not for you then? More interested in the golf are you?'

'Not at all,' Johnny replied. 'I love farming but I need to know whether I can make a living from it.'

'Of course you can if you put your back into it, but how much do you want it, Johnny?'

'Oh a lot, I love it, It's what I want to do.'

'Well that's good then, we'll make it work for you. I'll come down later this afternoon if you like and we can talk it through. Have a walk round; get the books out if you like. If you're going to be the boss you need to know everything. We also need to check out the commitment of the farm hands as well – Dan and Joe. We need to know where we stand with them. They're happy enough working down there, aren't they?'

'I reckon so,' Johnny replied, 'but I've never asked them.'

'Then we'll ask them,' his grandfather replied.

Later that afternoon his grandfather went down to the farm. Johnny was in the yard stacking some of the milk churns that had been returned from that morning's delivery.

'Hard morning?'

'Just normal, but it's still good,' came Johnny's reply.

'That's the most important thing as it's a hard job and it doesn't let up. You've got to keep at it. You have to earn every penny in this game. You see there's a bit of history here. I've been farming this land for most of my life and let me tell you, I know this land and those farm buildings like the back of my hand. I've earned some good money from this farm. Well that was until the foot and mouth came along in the late 50's. It devastated so many of the farms in Cheshire. It killed off everything - wiped them out. I did restock with a few head of cattle after that but I could never properly commit anymore. That foot and mouth almost destroyed me, so I decided to take on The Green Lodge instead. I've kept the lease going on the farm though, just in case. The foot and mouth's all long gone now.'

'That's a relief,' said Johnny.

'Oh yes, you've no problem with that any more. I've brought the books down to show you how we've fared for the last five years. As you know, we've reduced the number of cattle during that time. I wasn't able to keep enough of them fed because of the poor land but I never did anything with the land over by the far paddock. It's a bit rough and ready over there and proper drainage ditches need to be dug. If you're prepared to work on them, dig them out and do some repairs on those outbuildings for the cattle, then you could build up the herd on Stand Farm and make your money that way.'

'Well I'm keen to give it a go,' Johnny cut in again.

'You see I never had the time or the energy after that foot and mouth. My stamina's not what it used to be Johnny, but yours? You're a fit young fella.'

'I'd be ready for the challenge, but I'll need some help,' Johnny replied.

'Let's talk to Dan and Joe then, see what they say.'

Further conversations with the two work hands confirmed their commitment and Johnny felt rejuvenated once more. He now had a purpose. He would commit to the farm and to his golf as an amateur but he would work in the evenings in the hotel as well. First though he needed to talk it through with his father.

It was a week or two later, after Johnny had finished for the day on the farm, when he decided to pluck up the courage. He entered the main bar room. For once it was bereft of customers.

'Father, have you got a few moments? I need to talk to you.'

'Now son?'

'If you can spare the time father?'

'I suppose now is as good a time as any. We'll have to break off if someone comes in. Let's take a seat in the corner over here.'

'Well father, firstly, I want you to know that I do want to be part of the hotel. Things are getting busier here and I want to help you grow the business but the farm's important to me as well. I could help out in the hotel in the evenings, if that's all right.'

'Well, I could probably work with that but I really can't see any future for you over on that farm, son? Is it really worth all the effort?'

'I've spoken to grandfather about that. He feels the ditches need clearing in the fields at the back and if I did some repairs on the outbuildings as well, I could bring much more land into use.'

'Is that so? Sounds a lot of hard work and expense to me.'

'I've got the horses and Dan and Joe to help me as well. Grandfather still feels there's money to be made but I'd need to put in the extra work. I want to give it a try father.'

'And what about the golf then? How're you going to fit that in as well?'

'That's important, yes, but I'll have to put it on hold for the next few months to sort out the land and the outbuildings.'

'Well if that's what you want son, but you shouldn't be giving up on the golf.'

'I won't father. I just need to get the farm in order first.'

His father inclined his head in Johnny's direction inferring his vague acceptance to his son's suggestion. In truth he wasn't completely convinced but he was prepared to give him a chance.

'I need your commitment here though. The hotel's on the up but it'll only be possible if you can promise to be here.'

'You have my word father.'

A smile from his father signalled his approval.

As his father moved away he briefly hesitated, turned and looked back at his son.

'Hey Johnny, you know we should have a round together. We haven't done so for a while now. We need to catch up.'

'Yes that would be good father,' Johnny replied. 'I'd love that.'

The last few months of the year were busy times for Johnny. His first priority was to replace the rotting beams in the outbuildings. The work would come at a considerable cost but it was a gamble worth taking. By late summer, a settled, dry spell gave him the breathing space he needed to bring in the harvest before the rains came. With Dan and Joe's help he would work all hours to ensure a dry crop of hay was safely stored in the newly renovated barns.

Finally, there were the ditches to be cleared. This was the hardest task of all. His two work-horses should have been his biggest allies here but they were tiring with age. The job took longer than expected. Still, by early October, the bulk of the work had been completed and Johnny could now look forward to a farm with a far brighter and more sustainable future.

It was a good few months before Johnny and his father got to play their match. Johnny had been out practising ardently the few days before. He wanted to beat his father more than anything but it came around far too quickly for the hotel landlord. His work commitments had left his game too rusty. By the side of the old horsebox Jack looked on. He knew what this really meant to the two of them. He sensed there was more at stake than just a simple golf match. This was about a father and son, about respect, about identity and about a young man's future.

Johnny was getting so good now that he was giving seven shots to his opponents, a handicap almost unheard of. It was likely that his father would need each and every one. They shook hands on the 1st but by the 4th it was clear that there was only going to be one winner. Johnny was in scintillating form and his skill in playing the ball under the wind was reaping rewards. Hours of practice experimenting out on the links had enabled him to perfect a low running draw which he could control almost at will. It was an ideal weapon on this, a typical breezy Hoylake morning. Three birdies in the opening four holes would put him four up straight away and from then on he was never less than two holes ahead. By the 14th Johnny's father started talking.

'You know, Johnny. This is the first time I've really seen how good you are at this game. I've watched you hit balls, but I've never seen you play so consistently well. Jack's told me what you can do but you have a real talent son. If you need a bit longer in the evening during the summer to work on your game just let me know. The hotel, well I can cover things in the short term for now. We need to find a way of showing your talents off to the world.'

Johnny was astonished by his father's words. He had no idea what he meant by, 'showing off his talents,' but he was immensely touched that his father should say such things. He was a proud man and Johnny knew it took a lot for him to come out with compliments.

The match was finally over on the 16th but it was effectively over long before then. Whilst Johnny had won, in reality both had been winners that afternoon. There was a mutual respect between them now that would change their relationship for ever. Little did they know that it wouldn't be long before they would play again in a far more significant match than this father-son friendly.

# The First Amateur Championship

By late April and early May 1885 Johnny had the main bulk of his farm work under control and felt freer to set foot on the links. It didn't take long to dispel the memories of his earlier defeat at the hands of Douglas Rolland. With the pressures of making key decisions about his future lifted, he was back to winning form. An early success on the second day of the spring meeting was followed by an overwhelming win over Johnny Laidlay, a renowned Scottish amateur from North Berwick. He was getting back into the groove and the Ball family was now proving tough opposition for all would be challengers. Following competition days it was quite common for his father to throw out an open challenge, to anyone prepared to back themselves against him and his son. Few though had the nerve to take them on. They couldn't afford to lose the monies at stake.

The esteem with which The Royal Liverpool Golf Club was held within the game was rising but there were also those within the club who felt its status could be raised even further. In February 1885 Thomas Owen Potter, the club's secretary, would take the bold decision to instigate a brand new tournament - the first ever designated Amateur Championship. It went without saying that the club secretly hoped that their home grown talent would win.

Initial opposition to Mr. Potter's proposal was considerable as the cost of running such a tournament would be significant. However, he was a shrewd and formidable character. He was persuasive enough to push through his proposal and take the gamble that the money could be raised to make it happen. He was keen to ensure he got there first before other clubs could take up on the idea.

Before the championship began there was one major hurdle to overcome. Concerns were being raised within the club over Johnny's current status as a golfer. Should he be classed as an amateur or a professional? On the face of things his acceptance of the £1 in prize money in the 1878 Open would suggest he was technically a 'professional'. However on closer examination, it was realised that no formal definition of either the professional or amateur status had ever been agreed upon. Cleverly the club decided to set their own rules based on the length of time elapsed since a player had last accepted any prize money. Unsurprisingly, as Johnny had received his prize seven years previously it was considered as being from too far back. Johnny would be classed as an amateur and be allowed to compete. Douglas Roland on the other hand would not to be so lucky. His prize money had been won the previous summer, in the 1884 Open Championship, and thus was deemed to be far too recent. He would be ruled out.

Johnny's opponents in the competition's early rounds proved little contest for him. His focus had returned. However the next man up in the third round would be a different proposition. Johnny would be playing against his father again. This time the stakes were very different.

No father, son contest could quite compare with those that had taken place between Old Tom and Young Tom Morris. At the time they were the best players of the day. Neither Johnny nor his father could claim to be in their league, but there was enough intrigue here to attract more than a few spectators. The respect each held for one another was considerable. There would be few given putts from either player today. Johnny needed no motivation or helping hand from Jack for this match. It would prove to be an intriguing tie, for Johnny's father was no slouch at the game himself. Few players could have got down to scratch having taken up the game only eighteen months previously.

John Ball senior was a tall, stout man who commanded an unusual, pig-tailed swing which although unorthodox, was certainly effective. It had been the undoing of many at The Royal Liverpool Golf Club over the years. He was also one who wielded considerable power within the club. A committee man and an astute businessman, he was keen to put up a fine showing in front of his fellow members. However, this counted for nothing once out on the course. He would have to summon up fresh skills to overcome the challenge of his son. This would be a battle of technique, of guile and maybe the odd bit of gamesmanship thrown in.

Crowds had been milling round the entrance of The Royal Hotel all morning, sizing up each of the matches and placing the odd wager here and there. Many chose this one to follow. Mr. James Muir Dowie, the ginger-bearded club founder and its first captain, was one such gentleman. Suitably attired in a long, stylish mackintosh, he was escorted by two attractive ladies on either arm, his wife Mary being one and his twenty year old daughter June, the other. However, whilst Mr. Dowie may have been dressed for the typical windy, Hoylake weather, his wife and daughter were dressed to be seen. June was not only watching the golf this morning. Both ladies wore their Sunday best and were out to impress. Each had chosen light-coloured, long-flowing patterned dresses, hats fit for the queen and parasols perched on their arms which were challenging the most optimistic of all the weather gods. Today was an important occasion in Hoylake's social calendar and there were more than a sprinkling of potential wealthy suiters on hand to attract charming young ladies. It helped of course that June's father had the connections to introduce her to the right company. A day out at such a prestigious event was one not to be missed.

Whilst the women may have won the fashion contest, the contest out on the links had yet to be decided. The match turned out to be almost a replay of the game Johnny and his father had played a few weeks previously. Johnny got away early but his father pulled things back in the middle of the round. In the end the younger man was never seriously troubled and a fine approach to the 16th finally ended the match by a winning score of 3 and 2[5]. Johnny was through to the semi-finals against another prominent player and

---

[5] This refers to the margin of victory in a match. All matchplay competitions are played over a limited number of holes – normally 18 or occasionally 36. Thus a win of 3 and 2 means that a player has won his match by a margin of 3 holes up on his opponent with only 2 holes to play.

member of the 'Westwood Ho' Club in North Devon, Horace Hutchinson.

Hutchinson, the son of an Army General was two years older than Johnny but commanded the presence of someone a good ten years his senior. A tall, highly literate Oxford graduate who sported a distinguished moustache which more than matched his opponent's, he was a true 'gentleman's' golfer. This morning he was attired in a well-tailored, light green tweed jacket matched by golfing brogues that fairly sparkled in the morning sun. He seemed to have outshone his adversary before he had even hit a ball. Despite their apparent differences and backgrounds the two players had tremendous respect for one another both as golfers and as individuals. This would become clear from the many writings of Hutchinson in the years to come, but this morning, all the talk was to be done on the links. There was a golf match to be played.

Fine conditions with a light breeze greeted the two competitors as they stepped forth from The Royal Hotel. After swapping holes at the 2nd and 3rd, Hutchinson took the lead at the 5th. With Johnny pulling it back at the 7th after a stone dead approach, followed by wins at the 9th and 10th, the home crowd were starting to sense a treasured victory. He was now two ahead. However, just as Johnny had done against Rolland all those years previously, he began to let things slip. Unusually, he could feel himself becoming distracted and unnerved by the jostling of the crowds and the sighs that rang out after his missed putt at the 11th. The old doubts about his suspect putting technique had returned and Hutchinson knew it. Hutchinson walked faster, Johnny withdrew into himself. Within no time the home favourite had lost four holes on the trot and the crowd was becoming nervous. A classic cleek shot drilled into the wind from Johnny at the 17th rallied the agitated spectators to bring it back to one but sadly it was to prove too little too late. A final magnificent approach from Hutchinson at the last would seal the match. The home favourite wouldn't make the final and the officials, who had so hoped to be able to show off their talented son as the world's greatest amateur golfer, were to be denied.

The following day produced a final which never matched the excellence or the expectations of the previous day's play and in the end, rather than Hutchinson, it would be Allan Macfie, a local sugar magnate and relatively unknown rank outsider, who would win the inaugural 1885 Amateur Championship.

# New Tools for a New Challenge

A few months passed and it was on to St. Andrews for Johnny's second attempt at the Open Championship. However, yet again in another major tournament, he was to disappoint. Like so many before him and so many to come on this testing course, he struggled both on the greens and with his driving. The extensive bunkering that Tom had laid out on this ancient links proved too much for him and he continually fell foul of its costly traps. In the end he totally capitulated. In fact it was so bad that ashamedly, he didn't even bother to hand in his card. In time he would not be the only one to do so at St. Andrews. Advance thirty six years and Bobby Jones, the American who was to be widely recognised as the greatest amateur golfer of all time, would do the very same thing, also on his first appearance on this renowned links. For the present though, Johnny needed a pick-me-up. He needed his home comforts and his farm.

Maintaining a working farm was hard physical work but he loved the challenge. He could also be his own boss away from the hotel where he still resided and where his father ruled the roost. When he returned each evening his grandfather would still ask for regular updates on his progress. He would take immense pleasure in listening to Johnny's farming endeavours. Within months though, all this changed. After a cold spell that had unusually gripped much of the North West, the old man's health began to fail. Within weeks he was confined to bed. Finally in the early days of the New Year, he passed away peacefully in his sleep. Significantly he had agreed with the landlord that the lease for the farm would be changed into Johnny's name before he died.

In the last few years of his life Johnny had become increasingly close to his grandfather, but rather than dwell on his passing he was more determined than ever to instigate the changes that they had agreed. He would turn the farm into a thriving profitable business. It would be his long-term legacy to his late grandfather. It was this that would drive him on and which would allow him to turn his grief into something positive. Already the work Johnny was putting in was beginning to pay off.

By the end of January 1886 it wasn't only Johnny's golf technique and confidence that needed refining, it was also his clubs. His favourite club which had served him so well and which had proved the beating of many of his opponents, was in need of repair.

He knew the very man to sort it out. For once Jack was alone in his workshop when Johnny called in. It was unusual for him not to be sharing a convivial exchange of words with someone. He was a good professional and a skilled craftsman but there was little doubt that his charm and general good humour had made him popular at the club.

'Morning Jack,' Johnny called out.

'I'm in the back. Come on through,' came the reply.

'Got a job for you Jack. I need a new cleek.'

Johnny held out his club for Jack to examine.

'Yes it has seen better days.'

It was the mark of a truly skilled player that a small area in the centre of the club had been worn thin by Johnny's consistent ball striking. Jack put it to one side.

'I think I've got just the blade for you here Johnny.'

He planted a brand new cleek in Johnny's hands. It was markedly different to what he was used to.

'Try it out. See what you think. The Carruthers cleek they call it. See the back here, it's got extra weight. The way you strike the ball, it'll give you another ten yards at least.'

'How much do you want for it Jack?'

'Take it Johnny – it's yours. I know you'll put it to good use but a win in the next few years at the Amateur would be good enough for me.'

'Not asking for much then Jack.'

'Nothing more than you're capable of Johnny, that's all.'

'Let's just see what comes, but thanks all the same,' Johnny replied and with a chuckle and a shake of the head he walked out of the door.

The summer of 1886 saw the Amateur Championship moved from its birth place at Hoylake to St. Andrews. Johnny had only just competed here in the previous year's Open Championship and the course still held bad memories for him. He was determined to put these to rest. His game progressed well in the early stages but after scraping his way past Johnny Laidlay in the quarter finals, an abject performance against the relatively unknown Harry Lamb from Wimbledon saw him beaten far too early. The St. Andrews curse had returned. Out on the fairways where once the bounces went in his favour, he was convinced that the golfing gods were against him, causing drives to kick the wrong way into bunkers or leaving him bad lies from which he could barely recover. Once on the greens the feeling of being hard-done-by was becoming engrained on his mind and his putting woes returned. He was now telling himself he couldn't putt and as a result, he just couldn't. He lost at just the 12th hole. Yet again his fans returned disappointed. In the end it would be the debonair Englishman, Horace Hutchinson who would prevail to win his first amateur title and raise the standard for the English at the home of golf. Johnny's failure did nothing to dispel Scottish views that the young Johnny Ball was simply, more talk than action.

Johnny was now looking in every direction for ways to improve: in his technique, his fitness, in his outlook and even in the clubs he was using. The one part of his game where he especially struggled was his putting. Until now he had been convinced that his problems were more in his head than anywhere else, but like most golfers, he would start with the clubs themselves. As with his irons, he opted for a putter with greater weight to the head. He now had a club which gave him increased confidence to hit decisively through the ball. It would also help to eradicate the many inconsistencies in the greens caused by the growing rabbit population at Hoylake. Johnny had also left his full set of clubs with Jack for general servicing. Now refitted with new tanned leather grips and fresh binding, he could step forth to play with a stronger self-belief and with clubs that he trusted.

Whether it was the equipment or the increased confidence that the new wand had given him, it certainly did the trick as Johnny was totally unbeatable in club competitions at home in 1887. He won all six scratch medals for the year at an average of just over 80 - a quite remarkable achievement. This was something that no golfer had done before or was likely to do again. Despite all of these successes Johnny still remained the same quiet, unassuming modest young man for which golf was an immensely self-fulfilling game. His significant victories were never to be shouted about. Once the round was played he was ready to move on.

One evening after he had yet again wiped the floor with his competitors in the late summer meeting, he was approached from amongst the crowds in the clubhouse by Lieutenant Colonel E H Kennard. The Colonel was part of the very establishment of the club. One of its founding members, he was also a recent past captain. Now a somewhat frail gentleman he still had a twinkle in his eye and a trademark greying moustache whose fine extremities danced to every kind word spoken from his lips. His utterances were normally immensely entertaining and jovial. Johnny admired his ability to bring people together with his infectious personality and his wild exuberance. Ever the socialite he was a larger than life character, but Johnny would frequently baulk when the gentleman lavished praise on him. This evening from across the room he could see the Kennard whirlwind approaching and he could sense the usual signs of theatre in his eyes. On such occasions Kennard would naturally act as the main impresario. He was dressed appropriately for the part. From his left breast pocket could be detected the outline of a silver pocket watch held secure by its chain. An opulent purple velvet waistcoat was doing its best to hold back the many years of his overindulgences. In the Colonel's mind

Johnny had just played the leading role in the award winning play. He had emerged the victor. In his view he should now be ready to take his final bow. Johnny, on the other hand saw things very differently. There was no way he would be going out on stage to be admired by all. He had no wish to take the final curtain call. He was exiting stage left. He decided to sneak out the back through the wings and up the stairs to his room. In an instance he was gone. It was typical of this self-effacing, shy man. He never wanted any plaudits and he disliked the praise that would so often be thrown his way. He was content with his day's work but for him, once completed it was over. It had been and gone. For now he was ready for the morrow. Within a few hours he would be up with the larks attending to his herd. He would be playing on a more down to earth stage in the morning. The Colonel would have to find a more self-indulgent star for his next show.

With so many home successes achieved in 1887, confidence in Johnny's abilities had been renewed and it was now being matched by the sums of money being wagered on his prospects for the impending Amateur Championship. The contest had returned once again to its birthplace at his home course at Hoylake. It would take place in late September.

Johnny soon breezed through to the semi-final where he met Freddie Tait. Tait was a long hitting amateur and all round sportsman from Edinburgh. A prominent Scottish golfer, he was later to introduce golf to Sandhurst before enlisting in the 2nd Battalion Leinster Regiment. This was to prove the first of many encounters between the two golfers and both were nearing the peak of their abilities. On the other side of the draw, in their semi-final, Hutchinson, last year's winner had been drawn against Johnny's father. This raised the real possibility of an all Ball final, a unique prospect. Sadly for those watching it wasn't to be and although one down with two to play, Hutchinson took the last two holes and booked his place. It would be a Hutchinson, Ball showdown, but there would be little doubt who the locals would be supporting the following morning.

The repetitive clunk of the opening and closing of the carriage doors signalled bigger crowds than normal as they poured off the trains at Hoylake station before tee off time. Greeting them were the ugly structures of the chimneys and ironwork of the newly established gas works which overlooked the station. Those who alighted that morning had just one thing on their minds - golf. As the last of the eager throng made their way from the station platform from the 9.15 am arrival from Liverpool, the engine gave one last steamy hiss to signal its departure and steadily picked up speed before disappearing off on its way to West Kirby. For those arriving early it was only a brief five minute walk from the station past the cries of the newspaper sellers and up towards the Stanley Hotel at its junction with the main high street. This imperious building had been a bold and attractive addition to the town and was built to cater for the increased number of visitors brought in by the coming of the railway. It was also a further monument to the importance of the well-to-do landlord, Lord Stanley, without whose say-so none of the impending events would be taking place. The owners were doing good business. They were benefitting not only from the golf spectators but also from those who wished to partake of the coastal waters.

A few stopped off here for a brief respite before the day's events began, but the majority turned left, and headed on towards The Royal Hotel to await the emergence of the two worthy matadors. They would have a while to wait before events were due to unfold. It left plenty of time for the other important business of the day – that of socialising.

The fashions on display were elegant and drab in equal measure that morning. Players in knickerbockers strutted, brandishing clubs as marks of bold authority. Behind them trailed small urchins - caddies who were simply paid to follow and keep quiet. Women in laced hats greeted men in boaters or bowlers. Smiling, they bowed their heads and in return men raised their hats to acknowledge their greetings. Together they mingled and showed off their finery. The milliners and tailors for miles around had plied good trade in recent weeks. In the background bookies shouted their odds to lure in would-be punters. Despite Hutchinson's semi-final victory over Johnny the previous year, there were few who could get good odds on a 'Ball' victory today. However significant sums were still switching hands. The locals knew the form Johnny was in. It was inconceivable, or was it, that Hutchinson could win again, and this time on Hoylake turf?

At precisely 2.20pm the booming voice of the Royal Liverpool Club Captain, Alexander Sinclair could be heard bringing the crowds to order and the contestants to their starting gates,

'Ladies and Gentlemen, the final of the Amateur Championship will commence from the first tee in precisely ten minutes time.'

Johnny was a tall, fit young man by now and sported a debonair moustache that was quite the fashion of the day. In the appearance stakes he was not to be outdone this time around. Knee high, dark red socks were matched on top by a subtle light-check, woollen tweed jacket decorated with a white rose in his buttonhole. He cut a dashing figure as he stepped aside to allow the current amateur champion to take the honour on the first tee. Well-dressed and suitably stylish they may have been; it would be the outcome of play on the links that would be the truest measure of success today. As the two players shook hands, they saluted the crowds and touched the peaks of their caps in due deference to all who were present. In the words of the soon to be well-renowned golf writer, Bernard Darwin, 'the game was afoot.'

Hutchinson took an early lead over the first few holes and was two up by the 3rd. By the 7th though, Johnny had pulled the match back to all square. His putter was working its magic for once. His hours of practice had paid off. With the players swapping holes at the 8th and 9th they turned for home, again, on level terms. The tension was mounting. Johnny launched one on the 11th but found the bunker. Hutchinson three-putted, to keep things even. Pulled drives by both players on the next meant the 12th was halved in a poor six. Mistakes were now aplenty. The nerves were showing as they continued to swap shots on the 13th. The noise levels were increasing with every cleek struck and every putt sunk. When Johnny produced the shot of the day, recovering to hole from a difficult stymie[6] on the 14th, the crowd sensed their man was on the move. By the next he was. A perfect four on the 15th was too good for his opponent and he was now ahead – one up with just three holes to play.

Johnny moved to the 16th tee. From his top pocket he removed his handkerchief and mopped his brow as beads of sweat began to form tiny rivulets snaking down the side of his face. He tugged nervously on his jacket as he desperately tried to get comfortable. From the left applause rang out. From the right came the first of many encouraging cries. To him though, the loud cheering seemed to echo back and forth throwing him into a mild sense of panic. People were moving in ever closer, jostling, frantically searching for valuable viewing space, hemming him in from all sides. He felt trapped and alone.

Finally a small hole appeared amongst the maddening throng as the referee parted the crowds to reveal the narrow fairway stretching off into the distance. Up ahead, the dominant structure of his home, the old Georgian hotel and clubhouse, beckoned him on. He had played this tee shot on the 16th many times before but not in these circumstances.

His caddie prepared his small sandy tee. Slowly, deliberately he bent down to place the small white sphere atop. It fell off to the right. He repeated the exercise. Again it fell off, this time to the rear. He signalled to his caddie for

---

[6] A stymie was the equivalent of a 'snooker', in golf, whereby during matchplay a player's path to the hole is blocked by his opponent's ball on the green. In such circumstances, a player would be required to either loft his ball or to bend it around his opponent's, to enter the hole.

more sand and tried once more. The whispers in the crowd increased. Success this time and the noise levels dropped. Not a sound. He stepped back and laid his now shaking hands on his chosen club, the brassie[7]; one hand, then the other. The left was too high, slide it down. He couldn't. It was locked. The right hand felt freer and he used this to unlock the other. He reset his grip. It still wasn't right but he had to play the shot.

His wild uncontrollable swing was the worst of the day, straight out of the heel. The ball started out left at first but on taking a violent swerve to the right finished well off line and ended up in the field - out of bounds. Hutchinson took to the tee. A man of significant stature, he now felt eminently taller and bolder. He wasn't to be rushed. He took his time. As a result his backswing was slower and more deliberate. At the very moment the club finally reached its zenith, like a wizard concocting a spell, his wrists magically kicked in with their trademark corkscrew turn, unleashing a power that grew gasps from the crowd. Straight down the middle. Milder applause rang out.

Johnny now took to the tee again for his replacement shot. He had nothing to lose this time around. Again his hands refused to relax and free themselves from their vice like grip. His mind said focus and control but his body wouldn't obey. The downward motion was rushed and forced and devoid of its usual control. On impact, the whole of Hoylake heard it - an almighty crack. The ball progressed

---

[7] A brassie was so named due to the brass plate fitted to the sole of the club. The club was the equivalent to the modern day 2 or 3 wood. The brass plate would help to extend the life of the club by protecting its sole in the execution of the stroke.

a mere eighty yards, but his brassie was wrecked. A three inch long split from shaft to hosel gaped open for all who were close enough to see. It was now no more use than firewood. He directed his caddie to run ahead to the clubhouse to find Jack and seek out a replacement. Events were turning against him. The hole, for all intents and purposes was lost. Back to all square on the 17th tee. Two to play.

Who would hold their nerve the longest? His caddie quickly returned armed with new artillery and his spirits grew. The new club felt good, the weight, fine. He needed it to perform to set himself for a clearer approach to the green. Again the club went back but this time the hands slipped - the grip was too shiny, too new. It needed bedding in. He topped it but it rolled a good one hundred yards ahead. It could have been far worse. Hutchinson lay thirty yards further on, just off the fairway. Two fine shots by both players and it now became a putting contest. Neither could hold their nerve on the green. Both three putted and they moved on to the last - again all square. Could Johnny trust in his new brassie again? He couldn't risk it. He didn't need to. Out came the cleek but he pushed it right - bunkered. Hutchinson followed and found safe ground in the middle of the fairway. Johnny's lie in the bunker was dreadful. A wild spray of sand exited the bunker but no ball came out. He needed his next to escape first time. It did but he was two shots down to his opponent. His approach found the green but he now had to rely on a mistake from Hutchinson. None was forthcoming from the man who knew his time had come. A superb, flagside approach from Johnny's adversary followed by two steady putts and the title was lost. For the second year running Hutchinson would be crowned British Amateur Champion. Johnny had failed again, and this time on his home turf. What's more it was to the very same man.

Yet further disappointment then for Johnny. Words of commiseration were proffered in his direction wherever he went and he was always gracious in his response but he was still bitterly disappointed to have missed out once more. His unique achievement of winning all the club's scratch medals in one season, meant there had been little else left for him to win this year. This had been the perfect opportunity to secure the one title he desired more than any other and to have done so on his own course. It seemed a natural extension to all he had achieved. He had shone in all aspects of his game but for some reason he hadn't been able to deliver when it truly mattered. In those last few holes his concentration, his nerve had gone.

Behind the calm exterior he was determined to prove his Scottish doubters wrong. Like jackals they poured scorn over the English supporters who had praised their young star like no other. The Scots had yet to see any real evidence of his prowess. Johnny's loss in the final had polarised opinion. Most of his home supporters still believed wholeheartedly in his inherent talent but there were others, a small but growing number who were beginning to question whether he had that steely resolve to win when it really mattered. They also doubted his ability to bounce back from another disappointing loss. Away from the speculation Johnny kept his council and retreated to his farm.

# Breaking Through

Time away from the game through working on the farm over the winter had helped to recharge Johnny's batteries. It was sorely needed after his latest disappointment. On his return to golf he succeeded in shooting a record 73 at nearby Lytham St. Anne's and he continued to dominate in most of his home scratch competitions. Despite it all, the nagging doubts remained.

Back at Hoylake one late afternoon, as a fourth practised chip failed to match up to his exacting standards around the 17th green, a lone voice called out from across the putting surface to break his now failing concentration.

'Keep at it Johnny, it'll come good,' cried Jack. 'You've got the beating of that Prestwick course,' (this was the venue for the soon to be Amateur Championship). 'Remember ten years ago. You're a far better golfer now.'

Johnny looked up and smiled. Somehow Jack just knew what to say, and he was right. He had always performed well at Prestwick. The course suited his eye.

Three weeks later the two of them were repeating the same journey they had taken all those years ago. Cleverly, Jack had booked them the same lodgings as before. Familiarity and contentment in his surroundings could only be a good thing, he thought.

They had deliberately given themselves a day for Johnny to settle in when they arrived and whilst Johnny practised,

Jack took the opportunity to spend time with his Uncle Tom.

'How's he playing?' Tom quizzed.

'Ne'er played better,' Jack replied.

Tom took one long, slow draw from his pipe and inclined his head in Jack's direction. His beard had grown whiter since Jack last saw him but his eyes had become wiser.

'Is that so?' Tom replied.

'Without a doubt,' Jack returned. 'He's git that lang running draw back again 'n' he's controlling it beautifully. It's giein' him maybe twenty yards on his drives.'

'And how's his putting? Any improvement there?' Tom enquired.

'Aye patchy, but on your greens, he's got a good chance.' Jack replied.

That was enough for Tom. He was keen to bend the ear of his nephew to check on Johnny's current form. He was well up on the play of the local Scottish challengers, and in his opinion they weren't looking too good at present. He might well put a few bob on the young Englishman but he would say nothing in public. He had learnt his lesson from speaking out too soon back in '83'. Extolling the virtues of a non-native and worse still an Englishman, does little for your credibility in St. Andrews, even if you are a local celebrity.

The fact was that Tom could see so much of his own son, in Johnny. The two may have been very different personalities, but they were both masters at the game. Tom's son, Young Tom had passed away at too early an age and yet he had had so much to give to golf. Despite his premature death he had helped to grow the game by leaps and bounds in Scotland by virtue of his strong personality and through the sheer brilliance of his play. Tom subconsciously saw the same potential in Johnny. He had detected a real spark and never say die attitude in this young man. He had observed him from his very early days as a ten year old at Hoylake and six years later in 1878 at Prestwick. His nephew had kept him in touch with his progress. His character was backed up by an unrivalled technique for one of such young age. Johnny was now twenty five, just a year older than the age at which Young Tom had passed away. He was more introverted, more self-contained than Young Tom but he had that same resolve that could drive him on to great things. Johnny wasn't a professional and would never end up playing as one but with his mastery of technique and resolute manner he could attract a fair following. In Tom's opinion, Johnny Ball had the potential to be a leading figure to help grow the game in England, in just the same way that his own son had done in Scotland. The game was relatively new to England but it was just beginning to take off. With the acclaim that John Ball was now receiving, he could have a major influence on its future development.

Despite the many miles that separated Tom and Jack, they were still close in spirit. They communicated by letter on a regular basis, more often than not, writing on golfing matters both north and south of the border. As an avid student of the game and as one who had been instrumental in its rise and development in Scotland, Tom was keen to hear of the game's progress in the south. Clubs like Westward Ho in Devon, Royal Blackheath, Royal

Wimbledon and The Royal Liverpool had established themselves at the forefront of the game in England and in recent times had produced fine amateur golfers such as twice amateur champion Horace Hutchinson, as well as Johnny himself. These players were now beginning to challenge Scotland's supremacy in the game. They regularly played the circuit of the Spring and Summer meetings at clubs around the country and the intense competition had raised the standards south of the border. As Tom and Jack sat side by side quietly sharing their opinions, it was evident that their combined golfing wisdom could be matched by few others.

The Prestwick course had changed considerably since Johnny had last played it and a further six holes had been added to make it up to the now customary eighteen. However, those first few practice holes Johnny played were enough to bring back the positive memories for him of ten years earlier. Better still, he had been given a bye in the first round and the fine weather looked set. His spirits were up.

His confidence was indeed well founded and enhanced by a convincing win over Capt. W Burns in the second round by 5 and 4. Next, a third round match against J Mansfield from Edinburgh proved a tougher affair but his superb outward half of 36 more than matched that of his opponent and he was two up by the turn. Mansfield was a fine player though, and within two holes he had brought it back to all square. It wasn't until the 16th that Johnny was able to poke his nose in front again. He was more than pleased to win the next to ensure no nerves would be tested going down the 18th. He finally clinched the match on the

16<sup>th</sup>, winning 2 and 1. He was now through to the semi-final.

Johnny had prepared himself mentally for another tough tie the following morning and had slept well overnight. However, as things turned out his match against Andrew Stuart wasn't nearly such a tight affair. He never found himself in any serious trouble. In the end he played out a convincing win, 4 and 3 to finish the match on the 15th.

His opponent in the final was to be an all too familiar one, the fine Scottish player, Johnny Laidlay. Laidlay was an old adversary, someone he had beaten a few years previously. The signs may have been good, but Johnny knew all too well how fickle the game of golf could be. It could change in an instant. Laidlay had grown up with an illustrious mentor behind him, Bob Ferguson, winner of three Open Championships. He was a fine student of the game and had also adopted a new and unusual interlocking grip. This was later to be taken up by Harry Vardon and would become known as the famous Vardon grip. Johnny on the other hand made use of the more conventional grip of the day, the baseball grip. Their styles could not have been more different.

Laidlay was Scotland's best amateur player and had just beaten another tough Scottish competitor in the semi-finals, Leslie Melville Balfour, by the convincing margin of 6 and 5. He was in fine form. The crowds would be firmly behind the Scot and Johnny knew it. They could prove crucial when spectators thought nothing of kicking balls into the rough from seemingly perfect lies. This match would seriously test Johnny's resolve.

Johnny made a poor start when play commenced after lunch. His opening tee shot found the railway running parallel to the long, narrow fairway. He was one down with the match barely underway. However, within no time he'd pulled things back. His bold iron play came to the rescue once again. They were level again by the 2nd. For the next six holes both players played a game that was safe, if unspectacular - steady irons to fairways followed by approaches to greens which required long and assured putting to secure their pars. They matched one another score for score. It was compelling golf. On the 7th Johnny broke the mould. In producing his silkiest drive of the day he set himself up for an attacking mashie[8] to the green. He executed it to perfection and holed the putt. He was one up. Within no time he had taken the 8th and 12th after careless play by Laidlay and the title was within his grasp. Laidlay's head had finally dropped and his Scottish supporters, who had been so vocal until now, fell silent and drifted away. Standing on the 14th tee Johnny held a commanding three hole lead.

Sensing victory he went for the kill. A final four to Laidlay's five and the match was over. Johnny had finally won the Amateur Championship. At long last he had proved his Scottish doubters wrong.

No one quite believed it at first, not least the local Scots who were now notable more by their absence than their presence. The only spectators left as the two players walked off the green, were a small band of joyful Englishmen who were now celebrating an historic victory. He had taken his

---

[8] A mashie is the equivalent club to today's 5 iron.

time but Johnny Ball had finally delivered. Standing by the green watching it all was his biggest supporter, Jack, his face now a picture of pure joy. Even Tom was forced to look away. It wasn't right for a man of his standing to show his emotion, not least when it was at the expense of a fellow Scot, but he had sensed it coming. There were no scenes of jubilation from Johnny though. He knew better than to celebrate in front of his competitor.

As Johnny bent over to retrieve his ball from the tin, Laidlay walked across and offered his hand in congratulation. Johnny took it in return and accepted his kind words with typical modesty.

Walking off the green to the accompaniment of applause from his loyal group of ardent followers, Johnny proffered the very faintest of smiles in their direction and they knew he was pleased. It was followed by a nod of the head and a tip to the cap. He wasn't one to show his emotions, but beneath it all, he was immensely proud. His chest heaved a sigh of relief. The win had been a long time coming.

He was presented with a gold medal for his efforts and the impressive silver trophy which would reside in The Royal Liverpool clubhouse. It would be displayed for all to see as a mark of his golfing prowess. In addition, he was also allowed to buy an item up to the value of £8, (amateurs could not accept prize money). He chose a shotgun. He would use it on the rabbits, both on the course and on his farm. His eye for a shot had improved markedly since his initial feeble attempts with his father all those years ago. Within a few weeks the Royal Liverpool Golf Club had granted him and his father sole shooting rights on the course and the hotel lunch menu would soon benefit from the decrease in the rabbit population.

Back at The Royal Liverpool clubhouse the members celebrated Johnny's first major win as only they knew how. Pendulum Brown worked the keyboards like no pianist before him and with the large amount of alcohol consumed, Johnny's father had more than one reason to celebrate.

# Stepping Up

Johnny's win in 1888 had set tongues wagging. At long last the English pretender had proved his mettle to fight off the best contenders north of the border. Although Laidlay pipped him on the 37th hole to win at St. Andrews the following year, there was now a sufficient up swell of opinion that English golf should be taken far more seriously. More importantly people were starting to question whether amateurs in their own right might one day be able to hold their own against the professionals of the land.

Rarely had an amateur pit themselves against a professional in an Open Championship, so as yet, no one could reasonably give a clear answer to this question. The issue of money was unlikely to be a major one for the amateurs. Expenses would generally be paid and the amateurs at this level normally had the funds to support themselves in their golfing endeavours. More often or not it was pride that was holding them back. Why would they play if there was every chance that they could be beaten?

Amateur versus professional matches had been held in other sports but rarely in golf. In cricket, for example, regular matches took place at both Lords and at The Kensington Oval. Here the distinction between amateur and professional was notable by their titles: the amateurs were considered to be the 'gentlemen', and were billed on the draw sheet by the prefix of 'Mr'. The professionals on the other hand were referred to as 'players' and were inscribed simply by their initials. The differences were so marked that each had separate entrances to the clubhouse. Similar differences were reflected within the world of golf. No professional was allowed to enter the clubhouse but the amateur was welcomed with open arms. It would be well over half a century before a professional would enter.

There was little doubt that there was sufficient potential within the ranks to suggest an amateur could contend. Along with Johnny Ball players such as Johnny Laidlay, Leslie Melville Balfour, D. Leitch, R. Adam, A.M. Ross, A.F. Macfie and Mure Ferguson all had the potential to put in a fine showing. Others such as Horace Hutchinson, Harold Hilton and the Lamb brothers could also lay claim to have the quality required, but none had truly tested themselves against the professionals, not at the highest level of golf, not in an Open Championship. The call was out to the amateur golfing elite to put their names forward, but would they rise to the challenge?

Before all this however, there was the small matter of the Amateur Championship to compete for. This year, 1890, it would return to Johnny's home course at Hoylake.

Johnny's father would host a very special guest on the eve of the championship. After an eighteen year absence from Hoylake, Tom had decided to pay his nephew a visit and check out the form of the home grown star. The hotel was very nearly full and a late telegram addressed to 'The Proprietor of The Royal Hotel, Hoylake' had only just arrived in time to secure a room for the elderly Scot. Tom knew that a win for Johnny on his home course would help to confirm his standing in the game. Tom was also eager to see how his fellow compatriots might perform south of the border.

It was just after 6pm when Tom stepped off the carriage outside the hotel. He was one of a number to arrive that evening, all the passengers being fellow golfers or their supporters. The talk had been keen in the carriage on the short journey from Hoylake station and spirits were high. All had recognised the elderly statesman in the long trench coat with his bushy, grey beard.

'Who's your eye on to win this weekend, Tom?' quizzed one of the travellers.

'Oh there are many,' he responded. 'But it will be he who has the feel and the love of the turf who will prevail.'

His listeners were suitably impressed. They had had the privilege of hearing some wise words from the father of golf but they were still none the wiser as to whom they should back before the gun went off.

This time there was no young enthusiastic ten year old to carry his bags into The Royal Hotel but the greeting Tom received was just as special. Jack had been waiting in the porch area of the grand building as the carriage pulled up. The wind was whipping across the drive and although still a hardy Scot, Jack knew where his comforts lay on such a brisk day.

'Hey my friend. Hou ar ye?' Jack called out.

'Naw baud at aw, an whit like yersel?'

'Th' beard's a titch greyer,' Jack joked prompting a wry smile from Tom. In an instant they had reverted to the broad Scottish dialect that had been the norm for both of them for so many years. As their eyes met it was clear that distance had not dulled the fondness that each held for one another. Jack may have become more anglicised now that he had been in England for over twenty years but the bond between them was still there.

As before Johnny's father had prepared a table by the window and the two men whiled away a convivial evening catching up on each other's news and discussing the relative form of the likely contenders. They were more than happy to partake of the hearty food, prepared and personally served by the hotel's owner.

'And how's that Johnny playing? Has he got the beating of them all on his home course?' Tom asked.

'He's a good bet that's for sure but there's a young laddie too, Harold Hilton, a local member. It's worth keeping your eye on him as well,' came the reply.

There would be much to play for when the competition started the following morning.

Johnny made his greetings just as they were tucking into their desserts. A brief handshake and a few words was all that was needed. He wasn't one for small talk about the game and he knew only too well the attention that would come his way. However he was touched that Tom had travelled down. He knew it was important for him to renew his family ties with Jack but he was also sensitive enough to know that he had come down to watch him play as well.

'I'm very grateful for your visit Tom,' he said. 'I'll do what I can to raise the English standard.'

'I'm sure you will Johnny, but give a thought to my kin folk all the same. We can't have you shaming us all,' he replied tongue in cheek. His eyes lit up as he awaited the response to come.

'I care little when it comes to the battle to be won Mr. Morris.'

'That's what I like to hear, fighting talk. Good luck Johnny. Use your local knowledge wisely.'

'I will Mr. Morris,' and with that Johnny bade them good night.

The following morning an unusual sight greeted the dunlins and oystercatchers that clung to the edge of the incoming tide. As a hardened Scot, Tom was a regular early morning bather out on the sands at St. Andrews and he wasn't going to change his habits now he was on English soil. A quick swim followed by a fulsome breakfast was enough to set him up before he ventured out to watch the action on the links.

The signs looked good for Johnny as play started early. A first round bye was followed by an easy second round victory of 8 and 7 over D. Fairclough. This meant he could go into the next day's play with every confidence in his game. He also knew it would help to preserve his energies for future matches to come. His win now set up an intriguing tie with the club's new up and coming star - Harold Hilton.

Hilton's standing at Hoylake had risen considerably over the last few years. He had competed in the 1887 Amateur Championship and had done well enough to get through to the last 16. This was a fine achievement for a lad of just 18 years of age. As a promising golfer he had only just gained his full membership. The previous year, in 1889, he had won four significant medal competitions at the club - the Dun Challenge Cross, the Lubbock Gold medal, the Kennard Gold medal and the Milligan Cross. These compared more than favourably to Johnny's three wins for the season. For the first time in a good ten years Johnny had been outplayed. Hilton was now seen by many at the club as the one who could push Johnny all the way, both at home and at national level. Many saw him as the natural rival to the more established player. Johnny however, simply saw him as the next man to beat should the need arise. The two were now drawn up against one another in the quarter-finals and all those who attended were keen to see how the young challenger would fare against the older and more experienced golfer.

This would be a match of differing styles. For years Johnny's supporters had been accustomed to his free-flowing, elegant manner with his customary exemplary finish to every stroke. He was a slim man with a distinguished moustache who was brief yet courteous, to all he met. When playing, his grace was evident the moment the club started out on the backswing. His strike was pure and crisp and was completed with effortless ease. For the last few years he had begun to command the stage with his unfailing nerve and steely presence. He was the model golfer who never fussed, never flinched and who at any moment could deliver the killer blow from a low drilled cleek or deadly accurate approach. To match his stylish play he would more often than not be dressed for the occasion in his trademark red topped calf length socks, knickerbockers, a fitted tweed jacket with handkerchief, and to top it all off, a matching and well-tailored cap. That was how Johnny Ball, the 1888 Champion golfer was attired on this, the afternoon of 11th April 1890.

Hilton on the other hand was eight years Johnny's junior. From the corner of his mouth he pulled on a thin, smouldering cigarette. His light coloured, but loose, ill-fitting jacket was matched by white golfing shoes, suggesting someone more self-assured, at least in the appearance stakes. His swing was busier, less elegant and more energetic, his backswing shorter and quicker. He was a smaller man whose final flourish to an exuberant swing would simply will the ball forward rather than caress it, as Johnny would. His whirlwind follow through would see him fling his arms through to the very end of his swing. Such was the fierce energy with which he approached the game that his cap would often fly off in the execution of his shot.

The two had crossed paths before of course. They had attended the same school and ever since, Harold had been inspired by Johnny's prowess in winning title after title both at club and now finally at national level. Before then, there had been that chance meeting between the two when Johnny had tripped over the pram containing the five month old baby, waking him from his gentle slumbers. Now twenty one years later the two came together on far more equal terms; Johnny the firm favourite and the more experienced and accomplished player, Harold, the young challenger with the fire and exuberance of youth and a touch of jaunty swagger. Johnny was keen not to be tripped up this time around.

As Hilton took on the master shortly after 2.30pm, there was little to separate the two golfers in the opening holes. Whilst Johnny took the 2nd, after a half in five at the 1st, Hilton pulled the match back to level by the 5th. A 2 from

Johnny followed by a magnificent 3 at the 7th put him two up, only for Hilton to pull it back again by winning the 8th and 9th. Next, superb iron-play from Johnny at both the 10th and 11th put him back to two up. Although Hilton suggested a brief fight back, taking the 14th in four to Johnny's five, it wasn't enough. He was to bunker at the following two holes. In the end a trademark, low-flighted cleek from Johnny on the 16th, finally sealed the match by a winning margin of 3 and 2.

Johnny's victory was one which most had predicted. However Hilton had made a fine showing in only his third championship. There would be more to come from him in future years. All things considered Johnny was relieved to be through to the semi-final and to have dispatched an opponent whose unnerving style had proven a real threat.

This hard-fought match was merely a warm up for Johnny. He was in scintillating form the following morning as he succeeded in playing out a comfortable win over Leslie Melville Balfour. In previous years Balfour had been equally at home on the rugby pitches or tennis courts of his native Scotland and had been talented enough to represent his country at the very highest level in both sports. He was likewise a proficient cricketer. Today however, on the smoother putting greens of The Royal Liverpool Golf Club he was soundly beaten. In the other semi-final, Laidlay, now the current title holder, had outfought Leitch by one hole. This set up a final that all were relishing between the talented young Scot and the resolute Englishman. It would be an intriguing repeat of the 1888 final. Added spice would be given to this one as Laidlay had taken the semi-final match the previous year at St. Andrews. On that occasion he had just sneaked through in a tense game which only ended at the 20th hole. He had subsequently gone on to take the title. Both had therefore proven themselves to be worthy winners at the high table of amateur golf in each of the last two years. The significant band of Scots who had made the journey south was quietly confident. As for the locals, they were unmistakably behind Johnny and were desperate for a home win. The scene was set for an intriguing and hard fought final.

Strong southerly winds had brought warm and testing conditions for the players as they prepared for their early morning's play, but by lunchtime ominous grey clouds had begun to build up on the near horizon. The sound of distant thunder and heavy rain accompanied by flashes of lightning had threatened to sabotage this, the final showdown. Luckily they were to be spared. After a half hour delay play got under way just after 2.30 pm.

Johnny had a new air of sartorial elegance about him this afternoon. He was clad in his customary red calf-length socks, but he now sported a new grey, pin-striped tweed jacket and waistcoat with matching knickerbockers. His outfit was topped off by a plain tweed cap. He cut a dashing figure for the crowds. For one young lady it was all too much. As the players were announced to the crowd she squeezed her demure frame between the congested bodies encircling the gladiators and stepped forth onto the tee. With blushing gay abandon and to everyone's astonishment and delight, she approached her man, looked him directly in the eye and with the upmost tenderness, planted a full red rose in his button hole. Her actions drew the wildest of applause and appreciation from the crowd. Johnny was every woman's dream - the modest, local, swashbuckling hero. Whether he would prove to be the golfer's dream would remain to be seen. In the corner, clad in his long ankle-length mackintosh, Tom looked on. A wry smile spread across his face. From the corner of his mouth he took a long draw on his pipe. Johnny was indeed a popular man.

The frequent showers in the early stages of the match may have dampened the spirit of the spectators but they had little effect on Johnny's play. He was in excellent form and took the first two holes with ease. As he removed his ball from the tin the call went up from the referee – 'Mr John Ball wins the hole in four and is 2 up.' The announcement brought cheers and applause from all around.

At the third a fine tee shot from Laidlay succeeded in stemming the rising tide, at least for the time being. They halved in four. By the fourth Johnny was back in the driving seat once more. A near perfect three was far too good for Laidlay. A poor half in six at the fifth was followed by a fine tee shot on the difficult 6th from Johnny but his poor putting soon came back to haunt him again on the greens. For a hole he should have won he could only manage a half. Still, it had been a near perfect start for the Englishman. With a third of the round gone, he now stood in the commanding position of 3 up.

As they moved to the 7th bold cries of encouragement filled the air but they weren't for Laidlay. His tee shot was weak. The pressure was getting to him. Ahead of him Johnny was safely on the green. Laidlay now faced a major test. Before him, lay a cavernous bunker. The flag was another twenty yards further on. Protecting it were slopes left and right. No margin for error here for the Scot and he knew it. As the club went back, his timing was lost and the ball scooted across the green like a scalded cat. Within an instant he was four down and the match was slipping away. Two holes later and things had gone from bad to worse. A misdirected drive on the eighth from Laidlay and a long holed putt on the ninth from Johnny now put Laidlay six down at the turn.

From then on it was just a matter of time before the final curtain came down. A brief revival from Laidlay over the next few holes was not enough. Johnny finally sealed it on the 15th. He had won by the commanding margin of 4 and 3. After his third attempt in front of his home fans, he had finally won at Hoylake.

The celebrations began the moment the putt was sunk. The skies were filled with flying boaters and caps launched with wild abandon by jubilant supporters. A spontaneous chorus of three cheers filled the air. Johnny barely had time to shake the hand of his combatant before being hoisted aloft onto proud shoulders and carried off to a packed clubhouse. Even Jack, who for many years had become all too aware of the support afforded to his adopted nephew, was surprised at how the locals were celebrating. As he was to remark later that night to Tom,

'It was as if the dam of emotion had finally been breached.'

In a flood of joyous acclamation the locals were revelling in the thrill of seeing their son finally achieve the coveted prize on their home course. Yes he had won at Prestwick two years earlier but this time he had achieved the feat here, at Hoylake. In home competitions he had proved virtually unassailable. Now he had proved himself at the very highest level. At last the men and women of Hoylake could celebrate in true fashion. The bottled up frustration of three home failures could finally be released and nobody was going to stop them in their moment of celebration.

Over by the clubhouse Tom and Jack were forced to stand aside for fear of being swept up in the maddening throng.

'I thought the Scots knew how to celebrate.' said Tom. 'Is there something in the water? The crowd, they're fanatical.'

The scenes were indeed remarkable and it wasn't long before the presentation celebrations led to more chaotic scenes in front of the clubhouse. Tom and Jack were astounded at what they were witnessing. It was enough to confirm two important thoughts in Tom's mind. Firstly, as he had long considered, he could now see Johnny becoming a standard bearer for English golf, and one who could grow the game south of the border. Secondly he saw no reason why Johnny shouldn't be able to compete on equal terms in the country's leading tournament, in The Open Championship itself. The two would have to talk.

Whilst the celebrations carried on through the night, led by a rousing speech by club captain, Mr. Charles Hutchings, in typical fashion Johnny retired early. He would be up with the sound of the dawn chorus, working on his farm.

Tom and Jack took a late breakfast the following morning before the former enquired of Johnny's whereabouts from the proud landlord.

'Oh Jack will know where he is. He'll be able to take you to him but no doubt Johnny will be out in the fields.' John replied.

'Out practising already?' Tom queried.

'Not on the links, Mr. Morris. Out on his farm.'

Tom raised a finger acknowledging his mistake.

By late morning Tom and Jack had decided to pay Johnny a visit. They found the young champion hard at work in the cowshed.

Johnny's reaction to his success took Tom very much by surprise, but for Jack, who knew him only too well, he was just the same as ever. For Johnny it was as if nothing had happened. He was quick to thank them for their congratulatory comments but once done he was keen to move on. The milking was of far greater importance to him at present.

'Have you considered having another shot at the Open in June?' Jack enquired.

'Maybe,' Johnny replied. 'I need to be sure that the lads can cover the farm and that the grazing is fit for the cattle first though. There are a couple of the ditches in the back paddock that need clearing as well and there's the harvest of course. All being well, if I can get that in before I have to travel up, then yes, certainly. It depends a lot on the weather to be honest.'

It was typical of Johnny. Work, his livelihood, came first and that was always how he wanted it to be. For other amateurs, such matters of ensuring financial security were rarely an issue. However, for Johnny there was also a matter of professional pride at stake here as well. He needed to get his house, or more correctly his farm, in order first. There was no denying though that Johnny was keen to give the Open another shot and Jack sensed it. As they returned to the hotel he and Tom were confident that the young champion would soon be pitting his skills against the

119

greatest that the world could offer in the most respected championship of them all.

It took several days for the town of Hoylake to return to normal. If it had been within the powers of the council to award a public holiday they would indeed have done so and few would have objected. Hoylake had now found its hero and its townsfolk couldn't wait to back their man away from home at the next major tournament. Johnny would be competing at The Open Championship in four months time. What's more it was to take place on a course where he had already won – the Prestwick links on the Ayrshire coast.

# Bold Challenges and a Second Shot
## at The Open

Before the championship and away from the playing fields of Hoylake, the small matter of a challenge match needed to be settled between two of Scotland's foremost professionals - Willie Park Junior of Musselburgh and Andrew Kirkaldy of St. Andrews.

For years the rivalries between the two cities of Edinburgh and St. Andrews had been played out on the greens of these two fair cities. Golf at St. Andrews could be traced back to the late 1400's and in Edinburgh, to the early 1700's but much had happened in the years since, none more so than the development of the professional game. For years small sums had been competed for between up and coming players and Young Tom Morris and his father had been very much part of that scene. However, this challenge match was substantially different in one major way – the size of the prize sum involved. Willie Park, the current Open Champion had laid down a challenge of £100 that he could beat any golfer who would care to take him on. Willie Campbell of Earlsferry had initially put his name forward but the contest fell through at the last moment. The gauntlet had subsequently been taken up by Andrew Kirkaldy.

Kirkaldy was a tough competitor and soon to be soldier, who would fight at Tel-el-Kebir and Omburman, near Khartoum. A larger than life character, he was well known for his quick, dry wit and fiery temper. He would be more than a match for Willie. The fact that a professional should have the confidence, perhaps arrogance, to throw out such a challenge, typified the differences between the professional and amateur games. It was a million miles away from how Johnny saw things.

The match took on even greater spice as the two had tied in the previous year's Open Championship. On that occasion Willie Park had emerged the eventual winner by the narrowest of margins, via a play-off. The use of his goose-necked putter, a club which Willie had invented, had been crucial in that match but there was no saying what would happen this time around. The contest was finally on, and for both players it was equally a matter of finance and pride that was now at stake.

The overall contest would be played out over four courses: Musselburgh, Prestwick, Troon and St. Andrews with thirty six holes to be played on each course – a veritable marathon. A golf challenge of this magnitude had never before been issued. It brought keen speculation from those in the sporting world as to who would come out the victor. This interest was matched by the large number of followers out on the course, an average of over 4,000 a day. By the final day of competition, the links at St. Andrews was buzzing.

Kirkaldy went into the final round three up on his adversary but it was soon to be extended in the holes to come. In the end his final 8 and 7 margin victory was significant but judged over a full 104 holes it was relatively small. The crowd had been gripped throughout at each of the four venues and the interest shown had raised the public awareness of golf as a game for the masses. As Tom had predicted, golf was growing fast. The scene was suitably set for the start of the Open Championship in just ten days' time.

The field was a strong one as play commenced with only Douglas Rolland amongst the notable professional absentees. Johnny was being viewed very differently since his last appearance in the Open in 1878. He was a bigger threat. He had now won two Amateur titles, the last one being only a few months earlier. However, the competition was far stronger this time around. As for Johnny himself, in a rare reply to an inquisitive reporter he was quoted as saying that, 'a place amongst the first six would satisfy my aspirations.'

Naturally Tom would be playing once more. This would be his thirtieth championship and although he had no realistic chance of success his presence at the ripe old age of sixty nine was a measure of both his remarkable fortitude and his perseverance. There was a strong sense of stubborn Scottish pride in this wise old man. He needed little motivation when competing on a course where he had laboured and bared his soul for so many years. He had been keeper of the greens here from 1851 to 1865. It was here that he had perfected his skills in establishing greens that were pure and true and which would become the model for so many courses to come. Of the amateur players, Hutchinson, Laidlay and Ball had all entered but the keen money was on the professionals and on one man in particular, Andrew Kirkaldy, the recent victor at St. Andrews.

Prestwick held a long history of hosting Open Championships and was the first club to do so 30 years previously. Willie Park Senior, the father of the current Willie Park, had been the first ever winner of that championship in 1860 and he had gone on to win it a further three times. His son now trailed him by two. Smarting from his recent defeat from Andrew Kirkaldy, Willie was keen to get his revenge.

The weather wasn't to favour the early starters on the first morning. A strong north-westerly breeze had whipped up overnight and many were now suffering. Willie Park and Ben Sayers, both of whom had been highly fancied were among those to bear the brunt of the gales.

Johnny had been paired with Willie Campbell, a Scottish professional from Musselburgh who had come close to winning the championship only three years previously. But for a disastrous eight after finding a bunker on the 16th hole he would most surely have done so.

It was Andrew Kirkaldy who came out of the traps fastest on day one. He was proving his backers a worthy bet by notching up a fine score of 81 for his first eighteen holes. Following closely behind were Hugh Kirkaldy, Andrew's brother, along with Johnny himself, both tied on 82, and one shot further back, the confident Earlsferry-born player Archie Simpson.

Johnny's oily, grooved swing soon started to impress the growing band of enthusiastic spectators at the start of his second round. Whilst outwardly he was going about his play in his normal nonchalant way, inwardly his confidence was growing with every stroke. The early morning winds had dampened the chances of many and had improved his own immeasurably. The wild weather was playing straight into his hands. His low running draw was the perfect weapon in such testing conditions. His driving may have been solid but it was his approach play that had impressed the most. Time and again he was imperious in a way that outshone all others, laying his ball dead at the $2^{nd}$, $4^{th}$, $7^{th}$ and $17^{th}$ holes for scores that required the simplest of putting, the part of his game which had so often proved his Achilles heel.

The Prestwick links was well known not only for its mountainous sand hills, but also for one other significant hazard, that of the railway. This most unforgiving of all obstacles had been instrumental in promoting the very development of the game by giving players access to courses that would otherwise have been unreachable. Today though, it was to prove crucial in deciding the fate of many of the key competitors. At the first, the Cemetery, Simpson twice saw his ball follow the iron rails. He ended up with a disappointing seven, a score which he went on to match yet again at the Cardinal just a few holes later. Meanwhile up ahead, Andrew Kirkaldy was likewise faltering with a similar score on the $9^{th}$. In between, Johnny just kept his head down and forged a steady path that continued to keep those golfing demons at bay. That was until Monkton, the $6^{th}$. A wild second shot onto the rails here spelt what seemed like instant disaster, or so he thought.

As Jack looked on from the side lines his gaze turned upwards as if seeking divine intervention. Under his breath he muttered a few desperate words, 'Johnny Ball what have you done?' By the time he got to where he suspected his ball to be, his player had an army of supporters searching for him. There are times when popularity in the game can work in one's favour and this was one such moment. The legion of ball spotters finally brought success. The ball was found just before the final five minutes was up. The penalty for his misdemeanour would only be one shot as opposed to two. Johnny was still in the game but Jack was concerned. To him Johnny looked calm and collected but he had no way of knowing. He remembered the last time Johnny had faltered like this. He had been a young sixteen year old at the time and he had had no great ambitions of success when setting off on his golfing journey that day. How times had changed and how he had improved. He had courted disaster back then and had done so in amateur finals and semi-finals since. A broken club in the closing stages in '87', and the match had got away from him. Jack had been able to pass on brief words of encouragement to him on that occasion but not today. The scene had become much too chaotic to do so now. He could only hope that Johnny's experience and maturity would carry him through.

By the 10th his play had settled down. No mistakes since Monkton. The signs were looking good. By the next all those present were staggered to see his partner tear up his card and walk off. A desperate eight from Willie Campbell had been the final straw. On the face of it, Campbell's departure meant little. The competition was a stroke play[9] one after all and Campbell hadn't been in contention. On the other hand for Johnny it meant another unwanted distraction had been eliminated. He was now playing on his own. He refocussed. With just four holes remaining he

---

[9] A strokeplay competition differs from a matchplay one as it is decided on the total number of shots played rather than in overcoming one's individual opponent by the number of holes won.

knew what was required. Word had got back. Willie Fernie and Archie Simpson had both posted final rounds of 167. Johnny needed to take no more than twenty shots from here on in and the title was his.

Not only did Johnny know what was required, so too did the crowd. Those who had been following Fernie and Simpson now switched to watch Johnny. They charged over in their masses to follow the new favourite home.

Johnny stood tall and confident on the 15th tee as he looked out across the broken land and the patchwork of bents and dips that lay before him. The distant fairway seemed a long way off but his driving had been sure and solid until now. Behind him and to his right and left the crowds inched closer. Heads poked through gaps seeking every vantage point possible. The stewards finally called for calm and a hush descended on the scene. Johnny's club head gently grazed the turf as he slowly pulled it back to the top of the arc. It came through squarely and swiftly and the ball was safely on its way. Fairway found, his first objective had been achieved.

Remarkably Johnny would keep this form up for the next half an hour. For the remaining three holes his rhythm and concentration never faltered. A comfortable five, then a four and a reassuring five to follow meant he was almost home. He could take a six on the last and still win.

Following and hidden within the crowds, two fellow golfers looked on. Horace Hutchinson, one of Johnny's previous protagonists and Dr P.G. Purves, the renowned golf architect, couldn't quite believe what they were witnessing. With a mild shake of his head Hutchinson turned to his partner and whispered the words that he never believed he would utter,

'You know what, Ball is about to do the most incredible thing. Something that's never been done before. As an amateur he's about to win the Open Championship.'

Briefly and excitedly Purves replied, 'Horace, this is a great day for golf.' [10]

The crowds had swelled to ten deep as Johnny headed down eighteen. His tee shot, from the high vantage point was perfect yet again. He couldn't yet fully relax but he knew that one final, firm cleek would see him home. The crowd cheered him on every step of the way down that final fairway. His band of loyal supporters was out in force and in fine voice, but many locals were still unaware of the history that was in the making - an Englishman, an amateur winning the Open!

Johnny remained steely and purposeful to the end. He marched on. By nature he had always been a quick player and saw no reason to change things now. He reached his ball well before his caddie, but so too had the huge crowd and as one uncontrollable mass, they moved in ever closer. He was ready to play but his clubs still hadn't arrived. As the matador waited, a freak wind picked up and swirled around amongst all present causing spectators to cower and hunker down as hats flew off in every direction. For a moment, confusion reigned as people dashed one way, then the other. Throughout it all Johnny stood over his ball watching, waiting; calmness personified. At last his young

---

[10] Horace Hutchinson describes the scene as he and Dr P G Purves observe John Ball's victory in his Open triumph in his book 'The Book of Golf and Golfers 1899'.

porter arrived after a desperate fight through the mass of congested bodies. As quickly as the wind came, it died and the crowds drew in yet again, this time even closer. Johnny asked for space. People tripped and fell as some made way and others stood their ground. After what seemed like an age the stewards did their job and the spectators slowly moved back. The crowd finally settled and Johnny got ready to play. In the far distance he could just make out the 18th green encircled by hundreds of eager onlookers. Slowly, deliberately, he picked his weapon and set himself for his shot. A quick waggle of the club and with nonchalant, effortless ease, the ball was sent on its way. Up ahead the crowds waited in silence. Moments later, a light thud signalled the ball's arrival into the heart of the green. Wild applause erupted.

From here on in the march to the final stage took place in a cauldron of noise. The cheers were louder than ever before and yet this was Scotland not England. Johnny wasn't there yet but he was as near as damn it. His final putt dropped with his fourth blow. For the first time in the history of the game an amateur had won the Open Championship. Moreover, it was an Englishman who had done so and he was also the current holder of the country's amateur title. This had never been done before. It was a truly astounding achievement.

As the spectators cheered and his caddie removed his ball from the tin, Johnny looked out across the crowd and over towards the clubhouse. To his right was his past golfing compatriot, Hutchinson and next to him Dr. Purves. Both wore the widest of grins and were furiously joining in the applause. To his left he recognised Tom, standing firm as ever, wrapped in his long trench coat and trusty cap. He had completed his round a few hours earlier and had finished well back in the field but he wouldn't have missed being here at the end for anything. As their two gazes met, broad smiles spread across their faces. From the corner of his mouth Tom removed his pipe and raised it in Johnny's direction in salute to a player who he had rooted for, for so long and who had now achieved something that no other had ever done before. The two approached one another, masters both, and shook hands.

'Weel done Johnny, weel played 'n' weel deserved,' were all the words he could think of saying, but it needed no more.

Peering over the top of the eager crowd Jack looked on, tears streaming down his face. He had been emotional before but not like this.

It was not until a good half an hour after the presentation ceremony that Jack got to speak to Johnny. By this stage the crowds had begun to wend their weary way home and to the left of the green in the semi-darkness, they finally met. For a few moments not a word was said.

Teasingly, Jack looked down and pointed to the Claret Jug nestled in Johnny's arms.

'What's that you're holding my friend?' he said.

'Not sure,' Johnny replied.

The two hugged. Finally a few words came out.

'Let's see it then, this hunk of metal you've just won.'

Johnny handed over the trophy and together they stared at it before examining the names engraved on the base below. Johnny's wasn't there yet but it soon would be and it would now sit alongside the names of the world's greatest players.

The two celebrated in style later that evening in the bars of Prestwick before taking the train south early the following morning to Hoylake. It goes without saying that similar celebrations had taken place that evening back at The Royal Hotel. The Ball family had heard the news via a telegram sent soon after the final putt had been sunk. The main party had now been planned for later the following evening once their man had arrived off the Hoylake train. News of Johnny's success soon spread and the scenes were wild and exuberant when he finally returned. The cheering crowds were accompanied by fog horns and smoke signals in salute to their champion. His father had arranged a personal carriage to whisk him home. It would be drawn not by horses but by the blue-jerseyed fishermen who were so much part of this proud town. These were the ones who as lifeboat men would risk their lives for those stranded out on the open seas. They had so often been the heroes, but tonight Johnny was their hero.

The food laid on at the hotel was extravagant, the wine fine and strong. Rousing speeches were made in Johnny's name. Pendulum Brown entertained on the piano as never before and the songs sung were bold and joyful. Many were in Johnny's honour[11].

---

[11] The Royal Liverpool Golf Club has a large number of impressive leather bound volumes which contain cuttings and extracts of golfing reports of the day. These were painstakingly cut out and assimilated by the club's then secretary Thomas Owen Potter. The volume for 1890 contains a copy of the verse which members sang in honour of John Ball's evening victory celebrations after his success.

They included a version of 'Do you ken John Peel' for which the final verse was changed.

It sounded thus:

*Yes we ken John Ball and his modesty too,*
*His skilful play and his heart so true,*
*And his champion score of twice eighty two.*
*On Prestwick Links in the morning.*

The toasts were many, the celebrations exuberant, but it was all too much for Johnny. He was happiest away from the acclaim and the praise that was lavished upon him. He wanted a quieter life. He was happiest on his farm.

# Consolidation, St. George's and
a Home Challenger

1890 had been a magnificent year for Johnny – an Amateur Championship, an Open Championship, the St. George's Challenge Cup and three medals won on his home links. He was even rewarded for his achievements by being granted life membership of his home club. It was richly deserved as his successes had brought the club significant prestige. Now, with his win in the Open, Johnny's popularity had grown markedly. Numbers of visitors to the hotel were also increasing, and many asked whether they could meet the man himself when they came to stay. Few were successful as Johnny had no great wish to be recognised. He was also often away or working on his farm.

Johnny's father was immensely proud of his son's achievements. He was also just as pleased by the way bookings at the hotel had risen as a result. Many would call in just to see the trophies and for many locals and followers of the game the hotel became a point of pilgrimage. A small portion of the club room was redesigned to make way for a display cabinet which now housed all the club's trophies. Pride of place went to the two fine pieces of silverware which had never before been displayed together outside of Scotland - the Open and Amateur Trophies. Whoever was on duty behind the bar or in reception, would take visitors through to the inner sanctum where time could be spent admiring and examining every detail of the silverware. Most assumed that the larger of the two trophies was the Open trophy. How wrong they were. Johnny's father would take this as a cue to explain that it was here at The Royal Liverpool Golf Club that the Amateur Championship had begaun only five years previously. His chest would swell with pride as he waxed lyrical recounting his son's achievements. He would also take a certain pleasure in apologising to visitors for not being able to meet the champion in person as he was currently competing elsewhere. Mr. John Ball had a business to run and he knew how to market his biggest asset. The irony of all this, was that whilst Johnny's father revelled in celebrating his son's success, Johnny would do all that he could to dodge the praise and adulation that was thrown upon him.

Fame wouldn't change him in any way. Throughout his life he would remain a modest and private man. As an immensely talented golfer he enjoyed the cut and thrust of the game, but he valued the independence that farming gave him.

There were drawbacks to Johnny's desire for freedom. His father couldn't run the hotel entirely by himself. He needed a deputy and the obvious choice, in the frequent absence of his son was his eldest daughter, Elisabeth. Until now Johnny's sister had worked as a domestic, alternating between preparing the rooms in the late mornings and helping behind the bar at lunchtimes or in the evenings. This suited her well as it gave her a sense of purpose, of pride and responsibility, aspects of her life that had been lacking until now.

The lifestyle of a farmer was one of long days and early starts. Likewise that of a domestic servant in a hotel required hard graft and long hours. Johnny's and Elisabeth's paths rarely crossed, except occasionally in the early mornings. When they did the two would often make the effort to catch up on each other's news. On her days off Elisabeth would also walk over to the farm and help pour the milk into the churns, ready for collection the following morning. It was an excuse to get out of the hotel and to spend time with her brother. The two siblings had always been close. When Johnny won the Open there was no one who could have been any prouder than his sister Elisabeth.

The following year, 1891, was a relatively quiet one for Johnny. Both the Amateur and Open Championships took place at St. Andrews and he struggled. He failed to make any serious showing in either championship. His best finish was in the Open where he came eleventh. It was a big disappointment after proving himself on the national scene the year before.

In truth, this year his loyalties had become somewhat divided. He had just bought two new cobs to work on the farm and he needed time to break them in. His old horses were no longer capable. With these new animals, clearing ditches, ploughing or harvesting could now be completed with relative ease. Putting in the hours to break these two in over the winter was time well spent and it didn't take Johnny long to do so. He was a fine horseman. He adopted the same systematic approach to training his horses as he used to perfect his swing - slow and steady, with measured control. In the past he had occasionally lent his old nags out to Jack to help with maintenance on the course when things got stretched, but he wouldn't be doing so now. His new cobs were too precious. With these workhorses now on board, his farm would become more efficient by the day. Time spent out in the fields though, would come at the expense of his golf. He returned home with no silverware this year.

Later that summer Johnny was invited to become captain of the newly formed Leasowe Golf Club and he gladly accepted. He was a popular man, who was in high demand. The captaincy had its benefits. He enjoyed being able to put something back and helping in the administration of the game. He was genuinely interested in furthering the cause of golf at the grass roots level and he felt a stronger connection with the common man than he did with those who moved in the higher echelons of society. Johnny had played at least two or three times a year at Leasowe and he knew the course well. It was a fine catch for the club to have him accept the role. In time he would also draw on his expertise as a farmer and use his knowledge of the land to give valuable advice to the green staff when plans were put in place for the development of the course. The downside was it gave him less time to devote to practising and it clearly showed.

The man who did prevail in the Amateur that year was J.E. Laidlay. Johnny had held off the talented Scotsman to win the title only the year before, but this time around, it was another fellow Hoylake man who would end up pushing Laidlay all the way - Harold Hilton. Hilton was eventually defeated in the final but he had also put in a fine performance in the Open Championship as well, coming eighth. The golfing world would take note. Another talent was now rising from amongst the ranks of The Royal Liverpool Golf Club. Johnny had a new challenger and he didn't have far to look to find him.

~

The Amateur Championship of 1892 would be staged for the first time at the relatively new links of St. George's, in Sandwich, Kent. Johnny knew the course only too well. For the last four years he had made the long pilgrimage south to compete in the St. George's Challenge Cup. The competition had quickly gained a reputation for being the most important amateur event to be held outside of the main Amateur Championship. Johnny had won the contest on each of the previous four occasions.

For the Scottish amateurs, the journey south to Sandwich was far longer than for most, but few decided to stay away. Of the final figure of forty five entrants, almost half were from north of the border, a figure no doubt boosted by the generous expenses offered by the host club. The St. George's club had only been in existence for five years but it had already gained great acclaim. Designed by the esteemed golf architect, George Purves, it had been built with the backing of rich and influential London businessmen and had been established as a genuine attempt to rival Scotland's greatest courses. Johnny's recent wins had no doubt influenced the championship committee's decision that an English club now deserved to host this revered competition. More importantly, St. George's possessed a layout that would be worthy of a renowned tournament and few would dismiss the significance of a club named after the country's patron saint. It would be enough to raise the spirits of a nation that was now becoming a threat to Scotland's dominance in the game. In time the club would be given the Royal seal of approval. Within just two years, St. George's would be hosting the Open Championship. England now had the players and the links to truly rival their Scottish neighbours.

Once play began it didn't take long for the elements to start causing problems. Johnny normally took such conditions in his stride but not in the early stages. He had been drawn against Andrew Stuart in the first round. Johnny had previously beaten Stuart in the semi-final of the 1888 Amateur but on this occasion things weren't going to plan. Out in just 39 shots, Stuart's play had been in a different league to Johnny's. Despite the strong winds he was proving more than capable of outwitting all that the weather gods could throw at him. After halving the 10th he was lying four up with just eight to play. When Johnny missed his second to the 11th it seemed the writing was on the wall. Unbelievably though, with the finishing line in sight Stuart somehow failed to hold his nerve. After topping his approach to a relatively easy green he contrived to lose the next three holes in a row. By the time Johnny brought the match back to all square on the 16th Stuart looked utterly defeated. Johnny finally sealed victory on the very last hole. It had been a close run thing but he had scraped through.

Mure Ferguson was up next but again Johnny held firm. By the time he had narrowly seen off his old adversary, Horace Hutchinson and later Leslie Balfour, he had earned his place as favourite in the forthcoming final. He would have one last challenge to face. It would come in the form of his fellow Hoylake member, Harold Hilton.

Hilton had been cruising his way through the rounds on the opposite side of the draw. He had played well enough to defeat the defending champion Johnny Laidlay by an impressive margin of 5 and 4 in the semi-final. Now for the first time Hilton and Ball would go head to head in the final of a major Championship. It was the match that every Englishman had been hoping for and they would not be disappointed.

Back at The Royal Hotel news that their two members had made it through to the final was greeted with intense pride. The Royal Liverpool Flag was hoisted aloft as a matter of routine on club competition days but it was raised with vigour that morning by the Club Secretary, Thomas Owen Potter. It would be imprudent of course for him to indicate which way he wished the outcome of the day's events to unfold but whatever happened, he knew that the name of The Royal Liverpool Golf Club would be held in the highest esteem. He could rightfully feel immensely proud.

Many of the club members had decided to make the long trip south to watch the proceedings for themselves. This, after all was a unique occasion with two Hoylake members competing for a national title. Those who remained waited expectantly for the outcome of this unique golfing duel. Among them was Jack. Demand for his teaching expertise had become too great over recent months for him to justify taking time off to witness the events in person. He was well respected amongst the members and those higher up within the club and he was needed back at base. Unusually for many professionals, in Jack's early days he had been given permission to support Johnny in his first Open Championship in 1878. Johnny was only a teenager then. On that occasion Jack's support had proved a major factor in the youngster's fine showing. Now though, he felt the arm of the club more heavily on his shoulder. He was required to remain close at hand to provide for the needs of its members.

Inside the clubhouse two of Johnny's sisters, Margaret and Elisabeth, were clearing away the remnants of last night's excesses. They were well-loved and valued by those who regularly stayed at the hotel and they carried out their duties with a distinct bounce in their step this morning. Quietly confident in the outcome of today's match, they were already making preparations for the celebrations to follow.

Of all those in his family, Elisabeth was probably the closest to Johnny. She knew how much he would be enjoying these last few moments before the gun went off. It was here where Johnny excelled. He was a master of controlling his play and his emotions when going head to head in grand finals such as these.

As Elisabeth glanced up at the old wooden clock behind the bar, she paused briefly as she thought of the preparations her brother would be making before setting forth. It was 9.30am. He would be teeing off in just thirty minutes time.

It was at this moment when one of the hotel's larger than life characters, Pendulum Brown, bounded into the lounge and greeted her with his normal joie de vivre.

'Well, the two of them will be setting off soon,' he announced, rubbing his hands at the prospect. 'What golfers we have here Elisabeth and your brother tops them all, you know. There's no one like him out there. He'll carry that trophy aloft by end of play my girl. Mark my words. You've got no need to worry there.'

'Well I hope so, Mr. Brown. I'm keeping my fingers crossed nonetheless.'

She smiled at his reassuring words. It pleased her that like so many others at the club, he had her brother's interests at heart. It was not such a bad place to work, here at The Royal Hotel. As she said these words to herself her mind drifted away as she pictured the scene for herself of her brother preparing to play.

'Are you all right Elisabeth?' Mr. Brown enquired.

'Yes, yes Mr. Brown, I'm fine.'

'It's just that you looked miles away.'

'Just thinking Mr. Brown.'

'Oh, I wouldn't do too much of that. It'll do you no good at all. There's one thing you could do for me though. Mr. Dunn and I are going upstairs for a spot of billiards. Could you bring up a couple of sherries for us? That would be excellent.'

'Certainly Mr Brown.' Clicking back into reality, Elisabeth made her way slowly over to the bar.

Hundreds of miles away, Johnny was quietly perfecting his putting on the practice green alongside the club's first tee. To all who observed his preparations at St. George's that morning, he was calmness personified, knocking in putt after putt with a clockwork rhythm and nonchalance that oozed from every sweep of the blade.

In contrast Hilton appeared restless, almost agitated in his look and his manner. He tugged at the corners of his lightly creased jacket one moment, readjusted his tight fitting cap the next. Faint ash trails marked the spot where he had spent the last few minutes practising. He was a chain smoker to the point where the cigarette never left his lips the moment it was lit. His mannerisms may have been those of a man showing extreme nerves but his presence here in the final was testament to the many hours spent fine-tuning his game back on the links at home.

The two had met in competition before of course. They had crossed paths in the quarter final only two years previously. On that occasion it was Johnny who had come away the victor in a hard-fought affair. He had a few years on Hilton. He was the more experienced and more established player. For those who enjoyed the odd wager, Johnny was the favourite for today's final.

A large crowd had gathered to accompany the players round. Amongst them were many notable gentlemen including Arthur Balfour, the Earl of Salisbury and the future Prime Minister. Significantly Hilton's father, Ben, was also present.

Ben Hilton had so far been the main driving force behind his son's golf career and he was also a member of The Royal Liverpool Golf Club. He held a senior position at Crown Life Assurance, one of the major insurance companies in Liverpool. With his father's help Harold was now working for the same insurance company. In a city that owed much of its success to the wealth brought in by the shipping trade, Crown Life Assurance insured many of Liverpool's major seagoing vessels and the cargoes they contained. It was Ben

Hilton's day to day work that had brought him into contact with the rich merchants of the city, many of whom were members of the Club. His associations with them had enabled him to gain membership and soon after, to secure junior membership for his son. Many an evening had been spent out on the course, father coaching son, encouraging him, even shouting at him, to follow through to a full finish in the execution of his stroke. The net result was that many years later, Harold possessed a consistent swing characterised by a final flourish that was unique and highly effective. Few who had watched Harold Hilton over recent years could doubt his honed technique. With a determination to match he would prove strong opposition to the two-time Amateur champion.

Fair weather greeted the players as they stepped forth onto the 1st tee and a keen and knowledgeable crowd had gathered in anticipation of the match ahead. Johnny had hired the same local caddie as he had done on his four previous appearances here. Although not superstitious, he still felt that familiarity in his routine could only work in his favour. Johnny knew the course well from his previous successes here and he merely needed a bag carrier. He had no need for small talk or for words of advice or encouragement on the greens. He had the ability to size up most situations with relative ease, a skill which generally worked to his distinct advantage. Hilton by contrast, was willing to build a working relationship with his caddie. He knew little of the subtle nuances of the St. George's turf and was keen to pick the brains of his new companion for the local knowledge that could give him the edge. The two were engaged in constant communication from the moment they met. A few yards away near silence surrounded Johnny and his man. Their working relationship had been established way back and each knew what was expected of the other once play got under way.

The players swapped holes in the early stages but by the 4th Johnny began to find his form. Facing a blind tee shot here with the fairway hidden by the high dunes ahead, his only aid was a solitary white marker post 150 yards to the fore. As the referee called for quiet he composed himself and let his loose-limbed swing take command of his actions. The ball came straight out of the middle. However, the usual crack of club on ball was swiftly followed by yet another. It brought an audible groan from the watching crowds. The ball had struck a glancing blow off the narrow guide post up ahead, causing it to ricochet violently off to the right. He was too accurate for his own good. Johnny's skill with his cleek meant that such events happened to him more than most. He now faced a second shot from a buried lie to the far side of the fairway. Without a moment's hesitation he was into his stance and the club had started its graceful arc back and through the ball with perfect precision. The poor lie seemed to make no difference. A second arrow-like cleek was soon sent on its way and the ball landed safely on the green a full 160 yards ahead. To Johnny's left an anxious Hilton shook his head in total disbelief and from the corner of his eye his father looked on with equal incredulity. This man was a magician. Two safe putts were enough for him to take the hole in four when a loss seemed far more likely. Within no time at all Johnny had regained his lead.

Around the billiard table back at The Royal Hotel, the sherries had started to flow. The dignitaries were lining up their cues on a different, but more predictable green baize to that on which the golfers were holing their putts.

'My money's on Johnny,' Pendulum Brown remarked as he fired a ball across the table and into the far pocket, courtesy of a perfectly executed cannon.

'I don't reckon it'll be as clear cut as you think,' came the reply from his playing partner.

'Maybe not but he'll hold his nerve when it counts, always has,' he replied.

Mr. John Dunn took a brief swig of his amber liquor and brushed away his opponent's cigarette ash from the corner of the pocket.'

'I reckon it'll go to the wire.'

Back on the course it was as if the players were listening to the very words spoken by their fellow members all those miles away. Hilton had pulled it back to all square. There was fight yet in this young man.

For three holes in succession Johnny fired cleeks to the heart of the green. His opponent matched him shot for shot. Hilton's caddie proffered words of encouragement and admiration at every blow, whilst tucked in amongst the crowd Ben Hilton willed his son on, secretly and silently. It was becoming a war of attrition.

As the match progressed Johnny's unerring accuracy began to tell. Finally in the dying moments Hilton had nothing more to give. Putts which had dropped now scooted on past, leaving testing returns that jangled the nerves and drifted on by. By the 15th the end seemed inevitable. As Johnny's final winning putt rattled into the tin Hilton marched over to his worthy opponent and slapped him firmly on the back.

'Well played Johnny. Well deserved.'

Hilton was as humble in defeat as Johnny was modest in victory. No one had ever achieved such success before – to win the amateur championship on three separate occasions. Back in the early 1870's Young Tom Morris had won the Open Championship three times in a row to claim permanent ownership of the championship belt. Johnny couldn't claim that right for the Amateur trophy but nonetheless, his successes were a major achievement. Once again the amateur trophy would return to its spiritual home at the Royal Liverpool Clubhouse.

Back in that very same clubhouse 250 miles away Elisabeth and her sisters continued with their duties. They had no idea of the events that had just taken place down in Kent. Upstairs, as the smoke haze lingered over the snooker table, the sound of clinking ivory signalled the racking-up of points as the balls dropped firmly into pockets. The friendly competition between the two club members had become more intense as the alcohol started to flow. Their shots were getting wilder and bolder. Balls ricocheted back and forth in a frenzied whirl of pinball from one cushion to another. In their minds they were two wizards with their cues. In reality they were two tipsy toffs showing off in a haze of smoke and alcohol. The result of their game would be an honorary draw. They would decide to call it quits having outdone each other in a brash maelstrom of snooker cues and balls. Twenty minutes later Elisabeth entered the room ready to serve refills only to find the two gentlemen in a very sorry state. Slumped in the corner, snoring away, they were lost in a heady, alcohol infused slumber. Keen to prevent an accident in the making Elisabeth slowly prised the half-full whisky glass from Mr. Potter's hand before it tumbled to the floor, shook her head in disdain and left the room.

There had been no sleeping on the job down south. The outcome here had been clear cut. By the time the players returned late the following afternoon, preparations for the evening celebrations were well under way. This time the plaudits rang out loud and clear for not one but two esteemed and highly talented Hoylake members. In the end, another chapter in the life of the club had been written and it was an important win for a man who showed no apparent difference in emotion, either in success or defeat. Those closest to Johnny knew differently. Elisabeth in particular knew how her brother might be truly feeling. She was there as part of the hosting party for the celebrations at the club but she still had time to whisper the odd word to her brother in between the speeches.

'You've done all right there Johnny!' She remarked in mild jest. 'Don't worry you can slip away soon. They'll never notice. They'll be too drunk to know. Those cows of yours need tending first thing in the morning anyway.'

It was all that needed saying. On an evening when so many complimentary words were spoken, the few exchanged with his sister meant more to Johnny than all the others combined.

~

Johnny was content to swap the golfing fairways for the open fields of his farm over the next few months. He played very little golf during this time. Haymaking was his biggest concern and he put his two big cobs to work from early morning right through until the last rays of sun lingered over the dusty, open fields. He was keen to take advantage of these long, dry days. He had built a strong working partnership with his horses. They were his pride and joy, his livelihood. Whilst away playing, they were his biggest concern and the one thing that drew him back as soon as he could. Joe and Dan, his two farm labourers knew that if all else failed on the farm, they must take care of his cobs.

By mid-October 1892, it was time for Johnny to return to golf and by early June he'd been able to get some reasonable practice in for the next challenge ahead, this year's Open Championship. Controversially it was to take place at Muirfield, a club which would be hosting the event for the very first time. Muirfield had been chosen at the expense of the more established Edinburgh course of Musselburgh but the decision had not been received well by all within the local golfing community. Musselburgh had been the city's first choice on six previous occasions but it was only a nine hole course. The decision to play the contest over a full 72 holes now made it unviable as a tournament venue. Musselburgh's loss would be Muirfield's gain and it would prove the beginning of the new club's long and prized association with this revered championship.

Johnny's success in the competition only two years previously had captured the hearts and minds of the public and the younger professional talent back in England. As a result the entry list now contained a greater proportion of English professionals than ever before. Included were two players who were to have a marked influence on golf over the next twenty years, Harry Vardon and J.H. Taylor.

Johnny Ball and Harold Hilton, the two amateur finalists, travelled up in a confident frame of mind and were soon joined by a good following of English amateurs. Among them was Horace Hutchinson, now an experienced player who had twice succeeded at Johnny's expense in the very early days of the Amateur Championship. In this, the Open Championship Hutchinson was to make his mark at least in the early rounds. However, by the end of the third he had shot himself out of contention with an 86. In contrast the two Hoylake members were progressing well.

Johnny now led by two from Hilton with Sandy Herd, Hugh Kirkaldy, James Kay and Willie Park Junior, each respectively one shot further back. It was inconceivable that an Englishman could yet again carry off the cherished Claret Jug from under the very noses of their Scottish hosts. Or was it?

It was a nervous and unruly crowd that had gathered to follow the players home for the final eighteen holes. Absent this time was Hilton's father. Unconvinced that it was worth his while making the long journey north, he had stayed behind. In the end his son had decided to enter at the very last minute, taking the overnight train in time to allow him only one day's practice. Despite arriving in the wee small hours, his energy levels remained high. He managed to fit in three practice rounds before the gun went off. It would be time well spent.

Johnny got off to a good start but his impressive driving wasn't matched by his finishing around the greens. Shots slowly slipped away and gave hope to others coming up from behind. He finished with a final score of 308. The St. Andrean, Hugh Kirkaldy, was the first to challenge but his play couldn't better Johnny's. Next up was Alex 'Sandy' Herd. Yet again, the partisan crowds were left disappointed. He too came in on the same mark, on 308.

Further back down the field a young, talented Englishman was doing his country proud. Two holed short approaches on the front nine from Hilton had markedly boosted his early chances. When he quickly followed this up with four fours and two threes in the next six holes, he had placed himself firmly in the driving seat. The championship was now his to lose and he wouldn't throw it away. Finishing three ahead of Ball, Kirkaldy and Herd, Hilton would win his first ever title. England could now claim two Open and two Amateur championships within the last three years, both of them won by amateur players and both from the Royal Liverpool stables. Yet again England was holder of both titles. Ominously for the Scots, the two relative new boys to championship play, Vardon and Taylor, both finished amongst the top ten. It was a sign of things to come.

It seemed Johnny had finally met his match but he in no way begrudged Hilton his victory. It was typical of the man that he felt more at ease at the evening celebrations that took place a few days later at The Royal Hotel when attending as runner-up, than he had done previously as a winner. The congratulations were being directed elsewhere. As for Hilton he soaked up the praise. He was in his element. It was an impressive win for the twenty three year old who had finally succeeded at this, the very pinnacle of golf. He had pulled off the biggest prize of all at only his

second attempt. Golf in England and at The Royal Liverpool
Golf Club was riding high.

# Club and Golfer on the Up

Things may have changed somewhat at Hoylake; a shift, if only minor in the balance of the golfing elite but nothing had changed within Johnny's world, certainly not in golfing terms. Back on the farm however, things were moving fast. He spent much of the autumn months making further repairs to the outbuildings. Two of the main doors in the large farm building needed replacing and the roof required significant repair work. It was several weeks' worth of work. He completed the job just in time. Early November saw twice the usual monthly rainfall and was followed by temperatures that barely rose above freezing for the next two months. His efforts were well rewarded. He lost few cattle over the winter period and lost even fewer calves the following spring. Those in the golfing world may have been talking about the rise of a younger star within the Hoylake stables; Johnny was concerned more for the wellbeing of the livestock from within his own stables.

A significant departure from Johnny's golfing routine in the summer of 1893 was a trip to Ireland to compete in the Irish Amateur Championships at Royal County Down. This magnificent links had been laid out by his good friend, Tom Morris, and was one of his best creations. With the mountains of Mourne as its backdrop, he had skilfully crafted a challenging test of golf from amongst the extensive dunes that abutted this wild, Irish shoreline. It was a mere one hundred and fifty miles across the sea to Johnny's homeland on the Wirral. He made the journey by steamer feeling confident of his chances. Within a few days he had returned triumphant. He had won at his first attempt in an important tournament inaugurated just the year before. His prowess was spreading to every corner of the British Isles, from England to Scotland, and now across the waters to Ireland where the game was beginning to blossom on the fair greens of the Emerald Isle. This would be the first of his three triumphs in the Irish Amateur Championships.

Back home on the Wirral the rise in the prestige of The Royal Liverpool Golf Club had significantly increased demand for membership and the committee were keen to take full advantage. Ever the businessman, Johnny's father had extended the clubhouse a few years previously and had increased the rents as a result. However the decisions taken at the club's autumn committee meeting were to bring significant changes.

The discussions that led up to these changes were fiery in the extreme and Elisabeth would be privy to much that took place. Chairing the committee meeting for the month of July 1893 was Mr. Owen Potter. Ever the protagonist he had just one thing on his mind - the construction of a new purpose-built premises for the club. Johnny's father on the other hand would have more than a few words to say on the matter.

'I feel insulted that the very family that has provided you with a home, with a fully furnished locker room, with committee rooms, with bars, with excellent catering and social facilities, even snooker tables and a piano as entertainment for your members, should be left abandoned as if they were worthless. How can you throw away all of this, these facilities, our history, our love and support? Surely we deserve more than this?'

From the corner of the room Elisabeth winced and covered her mouth in embarrassment. She quickly laid the drinks on the table and made a hasty retreat. It had finally come to this. Her father saw his business, his very future and livelihood under threat and he was prepared to fiercely defend it.

'I understand your feelings Mr. Ball and as chair of this committee and on behalf of our members I wish to put on record our gratitude for the support you and your family have given to the club over the years, but times change. Please do not take this personally. We must move on. We must face the fact that this hotel is no longer big enough to serve the needs of our members and you must understand that should this club wish to continue to hold its place at the forefront of British golf we need to offer facilities that match its ambition. We need a purpose built clubhouse.'

By the end of the evening, the proposal had been voted on and had been approved. A new clubhouse would be built and in due course plans were put in place to make it happen. It was an important move by the club and by Mr. Owen Potter. Significantly Mr. Potter was also a full-time resident at the hotel. He was putting his neck on the line by taking such action. He was risking his own wellbeing, the very roof over his head.

In the first few weeks after the decision was taken his relationship with Johnny's father remained frosty to say the least, but in time matters eased. At the end of the day the tenant landlord needed Potter's business. He was also a key figure within the club and a valued friend and he could still help to bring visitors to the hotel who wished to play golf.

Times were changing and within just a few years, life at The Royal Hotel would be very different. As for Johnny, he refused to be drawn on the pros and cons of the move. In typical, but also in wise fashion, he kept his council.

~

The following year, 1894, brought new and exciting times for The Royal Liverpool Golf Club. The Amateur Championship returned again to Hoylake. Up on stage once more were Ball and Hilton, each with proven talent and playing at the top of their games. Both had won the coveted Open title as amateurs. They were now on show to record crowds of over 4,000 a day, of which almost all would be cheering them on to victory. The scene was set for the two home-grown stars to prove themselves in front of a strong partisan following. As a three-time amateur champion and previous Open Champion Johnny remained firm favourite both in the heads and the hearts of the Hoylake faithful. However many also felt that this might be the year that Hilton would step up and show his true colours. He, like Johnny, knew every inch of the Hoylake turf. Of all the Amateur championships to be staged at Hoylake, this was the one which had got the public talking.

Also coming up fast in the wings was the twenty four year old Scottish challenger Freddie Tait. A spirited and passionate player, Freddie had entered the scene a few years ago and was highly acclaimed in his native land. However he had yet to prove himself at the top level of golf.

He was the son of Professor Tait, a fanatical Edinburgh golfer who had used his son's talents to develop prominent theories of the golf ball in flight. Encouraged by his father, Freddie had thus acquired an expertise through ardent practice over the links of North Berwick and St. Andrews and would soon come into his own when tested in championship play. A tall, good-looking man, his dashing and charming manner had quickly won him many admirers back home. He had also arrived at a time when his country had found itself outclassed by their southern cousins. In addition, he was a keen and formidable player of the bagpipes, a talent which could always be relied upon to rouse the spirits of a passionate Scottish following. He was the golfer's young Bonnie Prince Charlie, out to wrestle the crown from the English throne.

Such was the golfing fervour that local schools closed for the three days of the championship. Scruffy, enthusiastic children arrived early and queued outside the hotel for the chance to carry a bag. Many were lucky. Most were just content to have a day off school. Few truly understood the game but they were still keen to be part of the action and to earn themselves a few shillings.

'They went to our school, them two,' they would say to one another, pointing in eager excitement at Johnny and Harold.

For those youngsters who did get bags, as soon as their player's backs were turned, clubs started whirling as they swung them this way and that, pretending to be the next Johnny Ball or Harold Hilton. Those who were unlucky enough to be caught by their players were quickly admonished. Misdemeanours like this never helped their chances of getting a good tip. Many jostled for the best bags. None succeeded in getting those of the two great stars. They were already spoken for. Johnny had used the same caddie for several years now, Old Bill Jones. Old Bill was in fact, only forty five and affectionately known as 'Oggie'. Johnny had made his acquaintance twenty years ago through work Oggie had done for Johnny's grandfather. Johnny had subsequently offered him the odd seasonal job working on the farm, mainly haymaking in the hot summer months. Over the last few years he had started asking for his services as a caddie on a more regular basis and they had struck up a strong friendship. It was an unusual one as Oggie was almost entirely deaf.

Out on the course Oggie's disability mattered little. Johnny was always inclined to make his own decisions in any case. Club selection and the reads on any given green were made by him and him alone. Johnny merely needed a bag carrier at first but in time he would find someone whose intelligence and good humour were more subtle than most were prepared to give him credit for. Oggie knew the ropes. He was always on time and would never let his man down. His wide, flat cap shielded a gnarled but angular face with a broad upturned grin that revealed a mouth long since devoid of teeth. Below a dark, now somewhat tired jacket, a stiff, white-coloured shirt embraced a sombre black tie. It was his mark of office. On meeting, a brief handshake and smile were enough for them both. The greetings, the rituals were always the same. The moment Oggie took possession of Johnny's bag and slung it over his shoulder he was set to go. For the next four hours they would be inseparable. They would work calmly and silently and would form a formidable partnership.

Directing operations on the first tee was Jack. Ensuring players were away on time was a military operation but he carried it out with his normal charm and good humour. His command of office was an old driver passed on to him by his father, George. The club was now somewhat worse for wear, but he put it to good use. He would hold it in reverse, club head in hand and use the shaft to hold back the crowds as he made his way through. Mr. Potter had nick-named him the wizard. With his now premature silver-grey hair and distinguished, upturned moustache he certainly fitted the part. The area in front of the clubhouse had become a natural meeting point for competitors and the public alike but when the human mass became too intolerable a few kind words and where necessary, the gentle use of his crook of office, worked wonders.

Everyone knew Jack. He had been a fixture at the club now for twenty five years. Many of today's competitors had been taught by him and they would never have got this far without his advice and support. A good number were playing with clubs that Jack himself had made. His popularity amongst visitors and players alike meant that he struggled to prise himself away from the briefest of conversations. As he walked over to the first tee cries would go out,

'Hey Jack, have you got a new putter I could borrow? The one you sold me's hitting them sideways.'

On hearing the words, a smile would light up his face.

'It's the man not the club,' he would call back and carry on by.

158

Jack had a job to do. He had players who needed directing on the first tee. On championship days like these he was the official starter. Behind the scenes, Harry Harte, William Rutherford and now a rather portly Owen Potter were the true organisers and directors of the tournament. To all intents and purposes though, Jack was the man on the ground, the one the players all knew and respected.

The weeks running up to the tournament had been tough for Jack. The club had made a number of new appointments including their first caddie master, Herbert Hughes. A new head groundsman had also been put in place and whilst this helped to ease Jack's workload, the result was that his pay would remain fixed at £20 a year for the next ten years. The new appointment was recognition that the demands of managing a course as well as being club professional and club maker were becoming all too much. Labourers had also been employed on a temporary basis to help with final preparations in the run-up to the championship. In the end the decision to appoint Hughes and the other staff was well justified as the condition of the course had deteriorated over the last few months. A significant drought had turned parts of the course into a near dust bowl. Things had also been made worse by the expanding rabbit population which resulted in many golfers being penalised for unwarranted poor lies or in the worst case scenarios, by actually losing their balls down freshly dug burrows. At times achieving a good score would be dependent as much on good luck in avoiding such hazards, as in accurate and skilful stroke play.

In the background and overlooking the course, the skeleton of the new partly built clubhouse bore witness to a club which was on the way up. Out to sea beyond the distant line of sand dunes, the newly built St. Tudno steam ship plied its trade, sailing back and forth across Liverpool Bay laden with eager day trippers bound for the seaside town of Llandudno.

In The Royal Hotel the talk the night before was of a clear John Ball win and the local reporters were eager to grab any quote they could from the local favourite. Many would park themselves in one of the two main bars hoping to catch a glimpse of the man himself before pouncing and tempting him with free drinks and offers of backhanders for the odd priceless gem. They never succeeded. Johnny was wise to their ploys and he wasn't interested. He would run a mile before speaking to anyone. On the eve of tournament play he would be down on his farm. It was where he felt most at home. When the time came to return to the hotel he would take the long way round by walking down to the beach and entering through the back door; anything to avoid the fuss. All the talk was simply irrelevant to him.

Within the hotel Johnny's father was in his element. He thrived on the buoyant talk of his son's chances and from the constant questions thrown his way.

'He's in good form believe me. He'll put in a good showing that's for sure,' came his reply to an inquisitive remark as he poured out a couple of lively ales and deposited them on the counter, his chest heaving with pride. Business was brisk. It had been so for a while now. Every room was full and the tables were packed with eager customers placing orders that his staff could barely keep up with. John Ball Senior's pride however, extended well beyond his hotel. He could still strike a good ball when the occasion arose. Whether he could play well enough over a full four rounds and whether his knees could still hold out, would be another matter. Time and his failing health were catching up on him.

The wind was brisk the following morning. It would suit Johnny's game. He was a master of keeping it low by punching the ball into the stiffening breeze. Few could match him when the wind got up. He was due on the tee at 10.44am but he and Oggie had arrived a good fifteen minutes early. His Scottish opponent James Goldie wasn't so prepared. He pitched up with a minute to spare having struggled to find himself a caddie. He needn't have bothered. Johnny soundly beat him, winning by a crushing margin of 7 and 6. Meanwhile Johnny's main adversaries: Freddie Tait, Harold Hilton, Johnny Laidlay, Mure Ferguson and Horace Hutchinson were sailing safely through.

Hutchinson and Tait were drawn against each other in round two and a hard fought affair saw Tait sneak through on the first play-off hole. Following just behind was Johnny's father, but he was in trouble. Finding himself with an awkward lie in a bunker on the 12th, his left knee had buckled beneath him. By the time he completed the 16th, now three down, the pain had become intolerable and he was forced to retire. He would leave things to his son from here on in.

Whilst his father was struggling, Johnny himself was cruising. Two resounding wins in the next two rounds followed by a nervy win at the first extra hole in the subsequent one had taken him through to the semi-finals. Meanwhile further down the draw, Hilton had firmly beaten Johnny's namesake, another John Ball (entirely unrelated), and had been drawn up against Freddie Tait in the quarters. A nervous affair saw the Scottish challenger through to the semi-final by the slender margin of 1 up. Before Johnny could progress through to the final he needed to dispose of another old Scottish foe, Johnny Laidlay. He did so with relative ease. He was safely through to the final but who would he play? Tait was up against Mure Ferguson in the semi - final.

Ferguson was a kindred Scot, a Perth-born stockbroker now living and working in London. He was fifteen years senior to Freddie and of broader girth. Few rated his chances against the younger, more flamboyant and talented golfer, but match play can throw up surprises. Throughout the ensuing contest Freddie never seriously competed. Drives that normally sailed down the middle were sprayed this way and that. He bowed out on the 14th. The final would still be a battle between the Scots and the English, just not the one everyone was expecting.

Following a start briefly delayed by heavy rain John Ball and Mure Ferguson would battle it out in cold and blustery conditions the next day. It would test every aspect of their games.

The 1st saw Johnny take an early lead as Ferguson bunkered. The story was repeated again on the 2nd and by the 4th Johnny was a commanding four ahead. He was strolling it.

As Ferguson's four footer lipped out at the next, he flicked at the air with his putter in instant frustration and cursed his shameful miss. Johnny marched ever onwards. The crowd roared their approval. By the turn, Ferguson had pulled one back but his head remained down. A disparaging cry went up from the back of the 10th. It was directed firmly at Ferguson. He turned his head in disapproval. He was fighting not just one combatant but the whole of Hoylake.

By the 12th he had pulled back another - two down, six to go. At the 13th he pushed one out to the right. The crowd were onto the ball in an instant, surrounding it, almost willing it on to a painful death. On arrival at the scene Ferguson took a few moments to assess his predicament. His lie was appalling. Could the crowd have trodden it into the turf? He had no way of knowing but he would need all his skills to salvage something from here. His ran his hands through his hair. Concern gripped his face. He looked up for inspiration but none could be found. Which way was the green? The mass of spectators was blocking his path. Amongst the catcalls and the jostling the referee finally intervened. Desperately he tried to clear a path but the moment he cleared one, the crowd encroached yet again. The Scotsman's patience was wearing thin. Next to arrive were the blue-jerseyed fishermen. Bold and brazen at times they had been given their orders at the start of play – keep the crowds back. Calmly they stretched out ropes between them, pulling them tauter on every pull. From amidst the chaotic scenes their cries of 'get back, get back' bellowed out above the seething masses. They were used to handing out orders. This was the way they were forced to operate when working their boats. It did the trick. Amidst the turmoil Ferguson finally had space to catch his breath and set himself to play.

Over to his right Johnny's ball lay dead centre. Ferguson played his shot. It landed a mere ten feet from the pin. He gritted his teeth and purposefully clenched his fist by his side. Could Johnny reply? A few moments later the crowd had their answer. He had found the bunker. As they marched to the 14th tee Ferguson was just one down. By the 15th Johnny's lead had evaporated completely. Ferguson had pulled the match back to all square. From a seemingly hopeless position he could win this. The small but significant Scottish following now started to find their voices. Cries of 'Johnny's beaten,' taunted the 4,000 strong, English crowd. They weren't best pleased.

Back in the Ball camp, Oggie was feeling the pressure. Twice he had dropped clubs whilst waiting for his man to play. It had had little effect on his master. Despite it all Johnny's demeanour remained solid, unruffled, focussed. They came to the 17th – The Dun. Both players hit solid drives and found the fairway. To reach the green in two even by modern day standards would require a mammoth blow. Between them and their target lay an evil, barren triangle of out of bounds jutting out into the fairway. Beyond that, and in front of the green, stretched a broad, gaping cross bunker ready to swallow up any ball which erred or fell short, even just a fraction. Ferguson played first. He was risking nothing. He chose the conservative play and laid up short. Johnny felt bolder, stronger, more confident. He reached over to Oggie and pulled out his driver. Hitting the target with such a club would be a feat worthy of a true champion. Playing it off a bare lie seemed almost suicidal. He hadn't been swinging well. Ferguson had drawn level as much by Johnny's mistakes as by his own successes.

For so many years Johnny's swing had been grooved to perfection but not today. The club usually went back and straight down the line of play to a full finish, like a train gliding along on highly polished tracks. The ball would never deviate. The train would never leave the tracks. It could never derail. Oggie, his conductor at the rear, had for years just collected the tickets, picking up and replacing his master's divots as he went. All had progressed smoothly, his divots always clean, always the same shape, always the same length. Today though, the train was disappearing down sidings from which there was no way out. Those discarded train tickets, the divots, had been scattered in every direction. The litter, the mess was everywhere. Johnny had no option now. His choice made, he just had to get back on those polished rails for this shot. No margin for error now. A couple of practice swings first; he was oiling the cogs, smoothing the wheels. Then, a moment's silence and intense concentration, feeling the rhythm of the engine, ensuring the revs were at perfect pitch, he took the club back and let out the clutch. Slowly he eased the club head into the perfect position. The engine, the pistons were moving in perfect harmony. No jolting of the locomotive here. The ball took off straight down the tracks, over the out of bounds, beyond the bunker's back, straight down the line. Not a sound from anyone, and then like the mighty release of steam from the engine's core, loud rapturous applause broke out. The 2,000 spectators encircling the green were welcoming the gleaming locomotive home. It was an astounding blow, a champion's execution and the shot that would win him the championship. Two putts and the hole was his – one up with one to play. He had stopped the rot but more than that, he had dealt the killer blow.

Despite a perfect four on the last from Ferguson, Johnny was on the green, already in the station. He was safely in the dining car sipping champagne. He matched Ferguson's four with ease. The title was his. The glory would be shared with the whole of Hoylake, and beyond.

Once his final putt fell, Johnny's demeanour never changed. Despite the cheering, the wealth of acclamation and the wild celebrations that followed, his modesty remained. Engrained into his character by his mother as a youngster it was just a part of who he was. Today he had fought harder than ever before. The world was his and yet the worthy champion batted not an eyelid. Within twenty minutes he had accepted the trophy for the fourth time. Gently, calmly he responded with words of appreciation to the organisers, to his opponent for his brave performance and to the galleries that had cheered him home.

From within the crowd a beaming face looked on, her head poking out from amongst the tightly packed galleries. Like all around her, Elisabeth was cheering from the rafters but her cheers were louder than anybody else's.

At the back of the green two gentlemen shook hands. One was far older than the other. He had just celebrated his 60th birthday. It was the perfect present. This gentleman sported a bushy grey beard, the younger man, a silver moustache. Johnny's father and Jack Morris were overjoyed. All they could do was grin from ear to ear and along with the 4,000 others, they joined in the applause. Needless to say the celebrations continued into the small hours. Hoylake partied for days. Meanwhile, Johnny returned to his farm.

~

Maybe the events that Spring had taken more out of Johnny than he had bargained for, as by the August of 1894 when The Open returned to St. George's in Kent, Johnny competed but disappointingly, he didn't contend. A 13th place finish was satisfactory if unremarkable. Of more significance was another English win by the young promising professional from North Devon, J.H. Taylor. It wouldn't be his last.

A month later in testing conditions once more, Johnny would add another title to his haul, winning the Irish Amateur Championship for the second time. As a match play golfer, simply no one could touch him.

# Hoylake Tragedy

Johnny may have battled the swirling winds to win earlier in the year but the elements would bring disaster to Hoylake later in December. Just four days before Christmas a severe storm hit the coast of North Wales and the waters of Liverpool Bay. The tempest of 1894 was the worst to strike in almost a hundred years. The storm hit overnight. With the silting up of the Hoyle Lake many boats were now fishing further out off the North Wales coast, in the very seas where the storm was to strike with greatest intensity. At the time almost 200 fishermen lived in Hoylake, owning thirty eight vessels between them. Luckily not all were out that night.

Fishing vessels by the name of The Stag, The Margaret and Alice, The Ruby, The Ellen and Ann, The Betsy and The Mayflower were all out on the seas, crewed by men from the Eccles, Rainford, Beck, Bird and Sherlock families. Just before midnight the flares went up. It was the call to muster for the volunteer lifeboatmen. It was a truly wretched night but they had to launch. The men weren't paid but they saw it as their duty to be there in times of need and this was surely one. All who set sail knew the fishermen personally. They would drink with them in The Lake public house, in The Green Lodge and The Plasterers Arms. John and Joe Rutter were the last in the lifeboat. Around their chests, crudely constructed cork lifejackets. In their hearts a fighting spirit. They would need to be stronger and braver than ever before on their mission tonight.

Sixteen men in an open-topped rowing boat. No protection, no cover, just their oars and their fortitude, fighting wild seas and monstrous waves.

'Pull lads, pull,' came the shouts amidst the roar of the crashing waves.

They battled for hours like men possessed, down through valleys of churning water, up over mountainous waves, every heave of the oar, a major test, a monumental effort. Ten strokes forward, eight back.

It was to no avail. The gods were against them, the elements had beaten them. No lifeboatmen ever wanted to turn back. It was a sign of defeat but they had no choice. They would be resigning their fellow men to almost certain death. Fifty, sixty plus men, women and children were waiting on the shore, praying for the safe return of those who were floundering on the hideous seas. There were many more back home, their families, and their close friends. The onlookers grew more desperate as the swells grew stronger, fiercer. All wanted news. All were praying for their loved ones to return. Their heads sank as the lifeboat returned empty-handed. Amongst those on the shore were Johnny and Harold.

The storm was intensifying, the winds picking up. High tide was in a few hours. On land the lighthouse shone its beam out across the waters. It glistened and flashed on the swirling waves.

'Over right,' went the call. The beam came round again.

'Yes there look, for sure.'

In a flash they had picked out a mast. Instantly it was gone but a brief sighting was all they needed. Out went the lifeboat again, the crew buoyed by the fresh news.

This time it hadn't far to go. It was The Betsy. All was frantic, chaotic.

'Grab him now man,'

A body was pulled aboard but it showed little life.

'Turn him over, turn him over man,'

'On your left, there.' They grabbed another.

As the lifeboat came in two men were still in the water. Johnny and Harold threw themselves in and pulled them ashore. Battered, beaten and barely alive the men were taken to local houses and cared for by strangers. All from The Betsy survived but others were not so lucky.

Across the North West a total of ninety six vessels were wrecked. The Mayflower, The Ruby, The Margaret and Alice returned safely but many of their crew were injured, never to sail again. Tragically The Ellen and Ann went down and all with her were drowned. The Stag was never recovered and her crew likewise lost. The bodies were washed up a few days later near Lytham St. Anne's. Amongst the dead were three from one family – John Eccles Senior, John Eccles Junior and Edwin Eccles. John Eccles Junior was just fifteen years old. Johnny had been to school with his father. Other well-known and respected families lost loved ones too. Joseph Rainford and Joe Sherlock never returned. They left their families distraught and penniless.

In the weeks and months that followed the town mourned deeply. Only nine months earlier it had celebrated the success of its greatest son. It hit the community hard. Mr. Potter, Mr. Dunn and others at the club had known many who had perished. Joseph Rainford had caddied for Mr. Potter on more than one occasion. The fishermen had worked as stewards and marshals at many championships, keeping order and helping to ensure the tournaments ran smoothly.

There was a strong feeling that something should be done, that money should be raised for the families whose livelihoods had perished with their menfolk. By Easter the club had collected over £300 but it wanted to do more. The fishermen of Hoylake had played such a part in the life of the club.

Until now the tradesmen and local artisans had been rewarded by being given permission to play in return for work completed on the course. However nothing had been agreed officially. On occasions locals still dug up greens and rode their ponies across fairways. A small group still resented the loss of the racing and the freedom to roam across the warren. That needed to change. This was an opportunity for the club to give something back to the town but also to prevent further nuisance vandalism. When on 18th July 1895 the Reverend John King was asked to nominate three local men who could form part of a joint committee to form a new Artisan Club, the names of Joe Beck (fisherman), Harry Eccles (grocer) and Joe Linaker (plumber) were put forward.

Within weeks the Royal Liverpool Golf Club Village Play was formed. Over two hundred local artisans were given formal permission to play on the course at restricted times. In return they would be expected to carry out divotting and other maintenance duties around the course. To this day the 'Villagers' still exist, albeit in much smaller numbers. It is one of the oldest artisan clubs in the world. In the coming years Johnny would regularly play in The Glover Cup against the Villagers, all of whom were scratch players. They produced some fine golfers. One of them, Joe Lloyd, started his playing days as a 'Villager' and after moving to France would go on to win the US Open only two years later. The new artisan club would in time become part of the lifeblood of the main club and the community.

The year 1895 also marked another milestone. The club moved into its new clubhouse on Meols Drive. It was a new purpose-built building with an entrance hall, two bars, restaurant facilities, a large locker room, a billiard room and an upstairs workshop facility for Jack. The club was making a bold statement to the golfing world, one which, in just a few years' time would enable it to host the greatest tournament of them all, the Open Championship. For the Ball family adjustments would need to be made. It was one that a certain gentleman would find hard to make.

# Accepting the Future

In the main bar John Ball Senior sat quietly on his own looking out over the course opposite. There wasn't a soul around. In a whirl of skirts and hats Elisabeth and her friend Jane tumbled down the stairs. They were looking forward to a ladies night out.

'Are you all right father?' Elisabeth called out.

'Fine, Elisabeth. You go on and enjoy yourselves. You deserve it.'

Elisabeth was briefly silent as she looked over at her father. He never normally sat in the chair over in the corner. Her friend nudged her on the shoulder. She was keen to get going.

'Hang on a moment, Jane. Father are you sure you're all right?'

'Of course I am Elisabeth, now you two get on your way. I'm fine.'

Elisabeth wasn't so sure but with a quick look back she tucked her arm through Jane's and they headed off.

As they finally disappeared, John Ball Senior turned back to his ale. On a wonderful, hot summer evening like this, the bar would normally be heaving. Not tonight, not for many nights now. His custom had gone elsewhere. There were still regular paying customers, holiday residents and golfers who had come to play and stay, but it wasn't the same, not like the old days: no Pendulum Brown on the piano, no banter, no atmosphere and more importantly, little trade. He shook his head and returned to the bar to pour himself another ale.

'Evening John.'

Pendulum Brown was still in his golfing breeches but had donned a smarter, more elegant jacket. He was never one to do things by halves.

'Just nipping over to the club for a quick drink. See you later John. Come and join us if you like.'

'Thanks but I can't I'm afraid. I need to be on duty here.'

'No problem. I'll catch you later.'

'Have a good time.'

And with that he was gone.

'Have a good time. Join us if you like?' John repeated the words under his breath. 'The good times used to be here. How the hell can I join him? I'm running a hotel, although you wouldn't quite believe it. There's not a soul here. Might just as well join him for all the custom I'm getting.'

He bowed his head and slowly rubbed his face in frustration. In years gone by the trophies that his son had won would be placed proudly on display in the hotel. Not anymore. Johnny had just won the Amateur again but the trophy was now in the new clubhouse. Visitors were taking their custom over there to see it now. 'They don't come here to The Royal Hotel any more,' he muttered.

He walked over to the open front door. His mind went back to the time when he stood by this very porch. It was over twenty years ago now. By his side was Jack. The two of them were gazing out over the course. In the foreground his son was chipping balls onto the green. Far away in the distance were two figures.

Jack had piped up first.

'Who are those two out there on the horizon?'

'No idea, but what other purpose can anyone have here other than to play golf. They'll be back in the hotel bar in a few hours' time, that's for sure.'

That was then but not now, John thought. They would be returning to the new clubhouse now, taking their tales and their custom there, not here.

As he looked out across the links the scene was one of gentle serenity. The gorse was alive with insects buzzing and the air resplendent with the sound of skylarks chirring up on high before dropping like stones to the ground. In the distance the dunes shimmered in the heat haze and every few minutes there was the gentle clunk of wood on ball, in years gone by, the perfect scene. Not today. John Ball Senior's life had been golf, the hotel, the business, the camaraderie, the helter skelter of it all. He had a purpose and a status. What now in the fading years of his life?

He wasn't the sort of man to give up. It wasn't in his nature. He was tougher, stronger than that but his pride had been dented.

It wasn't only Elisabeth who had noted her father's change in mood. Likewise Johnny had also sensed it and it was beginning to affect the whole household. As he called in to the bar late one evening after returning from the farm, there was his father, again sitting in that same chair by the window, head propped up on his arm.

'Playing tomorrow father?' he called across.

'No, too much to do,' came the reply.

'Surely you're not that busy at the moment. Get yourself out there.'

'Oh, I am you know, this and that.'

A quizzical frown spread across Johnny's face. Unusual, he thought as he went upstairs.

Johnny wasn't due to tee off until later in the afternoon of the following day for his monthly medal competition, so when he bumped into his sister on the stairs, for once he had a few moments to spare.

'Father seems a bit down,' he said. 'I've never known him not to play in the medal competition.'

'He's been like that for a few days now, Johnny. Mr. Potter's asked him twice if he wanted to go up to the club for a drink and he's declined each time. That clubhouse has been open six months now and he's been up only once and that was for the grand opening. He's finding it hard to cope.'

'Yes but he's got to accept it. He's got no choice. He's got to get on with life. That's how it is.'

'He can't bring himself to Johnny. Downstairs, even all those lockers in the old clubroom, he's never moved them. Those old competition boards, they're still there. The dust, the smell in there, it's awful. I can't bear him being so lacklustre. I'm getting fed up with it.'

A few weeks later, Elisabeth bumped into Mr. Potter as she was cleaning the stairs.

'Mr Potter. Can I ask your opinion?'

'Yes certainly young lady.'

'You know my father. How does he seem to you?'

He was somewhat taken aback by Elisabeth's question and briefly raised his head in contemplation.

'How does he seem to me? Well a bit quieter of late I suppose. Still the same John Ball I know but perhaps a bit slower than he used to be. He maybe hasn't got the same get up and go that he once had. But then we're all getting a little bit older now aren't we, except for you of course Elisabeth.'

He smiled in her direction.

'You're very kind, Mr. Potter, but really, how do you think he is in himself?'

'I suppose if I'm honest he doesn't seem to want to join in with those in the club any more. Not like he used to. I should really know shouldn't I? We go back a few years your father and I. I've known him longer that I would like to admit. Yes, I suppose he's been a bit more subdued of late.'

'Exactly my thoughts as well Mr. Potter, and I have an idea. What do you think about this...?'

With his approval a plan would be put in place and a date for late November penned into his diary and those of many others.

Before then the golfing calendar was full and not just here at Hoylake.

# St. Andrews Awaits

Later that summer the Amateur Championship would return to the most treasured of all golf clubs - St. Andrews. It was a venue that still haunted Johnny but he was still up for the challenge. He would book his passage north.

Taking the overnight train he arrived early in the morning and was pleased to be able to spend a couple of hours over a meal and a few ales with Tom before the tournament began. He was keen to seek his advice on how to play the course. Of anyone, Tom was the one to ask. He maintained it. He nurtured it. Inch by inch, foot by foot, spade by spade he had put his heart and soul into that course. It had been a few years since they had last met. Neither had changed in any way. The tobacco stains on Tom's beard had got fractionally darker, his movement a little slower but nothing more.

Tom liked Johnny's reserve, his modesty. It came as a contrast to the brashness and at times vulgarity of many of the professionals he usually worked with. As they settled down Johnny started to quiz Tom about the state of the links.

'So have you put any new bunkers in to catch us out since I last visited?'

Tom could see Johnny's analytical mind working overtime.

'No nothing's changed. You won't find any new hazards there that you don't know about.'

'Don't want any of those geranium beds that we're getting all over the place now,' Johnny replied.

Tom laughed at his description. Both gentlemen had travelled the length and breadth of the British Isles enough to know what he meant by the term 'geranium beds' – the springing up of long, shallow, cross bunkers that appeared out of context with the overall layout of the course. Johnny despised such 'modernisms' as he called them. The two were very much traditionalists in their approach to links design.

Johnny's comment brought a wry chuckle from Tom and a light-hearted tug on Johnny's shoulder.

'You won't find any of them creeping onto any of my courses, don't you worry my friend.' Their eyes met and they laughed together.

'And what of my nephew, any news?'

It wasn't until past ten o'clock that the two went their separate ways, but not before Tom had slipped Johnny a note. As he did so he pointed to the words scribbled in the corner.

'Take this Johnny. This man is the best caddie in the whole of St. Andrews. If anyone knows how to play the Old Course, Charlie does. I've arranged for him to meet you by the tee at 9.30 am, half an hour before you're due off. I know you play your own game but listen to him, believe me, he knows his stuff.'

A nod and a firm handshake from Johnny were enough to show his appreciation for what Tom had done. He would take note.

The following day Johnny eased through the early rounds. Maybe he was beginning to understand how the

Old Course ticked. Sensibly, he had listened to Charlie and had stayed clear of the many cavernous bunkers.

'Ye juist dinnae want to go right 'ere,' he'd say on the 10th and 11th. Sure enough Johnny played left and kept out of trouble. The partnership was working.

In the quarter final Johnny eliminated Alex Simpson with ease. It now threw up an intriguing tie against his Scottish rival Freddie Tait.

The press needed little excuse to build up this match. Freddie was still seen as Scotland's big hope, the young darling, the bagpipe-playing soldier who could conjure up the deep-seated passions inherent in most ardent Scots. John Ball, in their opinion, exuded everything that was archetypally English. Smartly dressed and showing little emotion, they saw him as the classic, stiff upper lipped Englishman. In reality he was anything but. He was cordial, if quiet, modest and restrained. He was gracious to all, cutting when needed. Frustratingly for the Scots he was also a fine golfer and today he proved himself to be infinitely better than Freddie. Shots that soared to pristine greens silenced the crowds and would leave his opponent exposed and wanting. Johnny soundly beat him. He was through to the final. The only consolation for Freddie's supporters was that they still had a fellow Scot to cheer on, another Edinburgh man, Leslie Balfour Melville.

The two players had previous history. Johnny had drawn Balfour Melville in the semi-finals of the 1890 amateur five years earlier and he had beaten him comfortably. Three years later Johnny had been victorious again in the final at St. Georges in Kent, but that was then. This was now.

Once the final match got underway, Johnny won the first three holes with ruthless authority. It was the best way to silence the highly partisan crowds but his lead didn't last long. By the 10th they were again all square. As they stood on the 17th tee Balfour Melville had pulled ahead. He was now two up with just two to play. A half at either hole would suffice. The 17th was the renowned 'Road Hole', made famous by the cavernous bunker that flanked the narrow green. Balfour Melville's approach was on line but at the last it turned left and trickled in. Like so many before him Balfour Melville had committed the cardinal sin. Johnny bettered his six with a five - one down, with one to play. Somehow Johnny contrived a win on the 18th. As the crowds grew restless it was on to the 1st, their 19th and a playoff hole.

By this stage the whole of St. Andrews had turned out to watch the drama unfolding. The tall four and five storey buildings that flanked two sides of the hole formed a natural amphitheatre, the perfect setting. From every angle the faintest of sounds were magnified many times over and were transmitted back to the players on stage.

Johnny was first to play his approach. At the top of his swing someone coughed. He never heard it. Both players played short of the burn in two. Balfour Melville was up next to play his third and safely found the green. More coughing in the crowds; the infection was spreading. Johnny took out his pitching mashie, a club designed to give him loft. He had to clear the burn but he rarely used this club. He normally favoured the lower punch shot. This time he was choosing a different approach. The club went back but the wind got up. As the ball slowly climbed, it visibly stalled. At the top of the arc it faltered and fell, finding a watery grave like many before. Was it the will of the natives that drew it up short? In that single shot his hopes finally floated away and sunk below the silt at the bottom of the Swilcan Burn. The wailing cries of the gulls seemed to echo Johnny's despair. In contrast the jubilant yells and cheers of the Scots echoed round the streets of St. Andrews for what seemed like an eternity. If Johnny had pulled off the shot of the championship last year, he had failed miserably this time around. He had come up woefully short. Scotland saluted their worthy winner. The curse of St. Andrews had struck again.

The Glasgow Herald reported the news thus:

'The reputation of St. Andrews golf has been maintained even against the greatest amateur golfer of the time.'

By morning they couldn't print enough copies. In later editions they went further to espouse the virtue of their man. He was:

'As fine an athlete as could be found in Scotland today.'

One could sense Scottish readers filling their chests with swelling pride. The English sword bearer had been slain.

# A Family Celebration

Disappointment then for Johnny, but just a few months later his country would get its revenge. J.H. Taylor would once more steal the professional crown from beneath the Scots very noses. He would better the home-grown Sandy Herd at St. Andrews by a full four shots, to win his second Open Championship in two years.

Johnny's recent failure would do little to pull his father out of his sombre mood but maybe something else just might. The date for John Ball Senior's 60th birthday party had arrived. It had been penned into everyone's diaries for many months. Johnny's father knew little about it until the afternoon. His mood had lifted somewhat, as strangely, bookings were up considerably at the hotel that weekend. All who visited had been sworn to secrecy but the game was up when Tom arrived. He had given a false name when he telegrammed through his request for a reservation but there was no mistaking his presence when he arrived. It was difficult to hide a man like Tom Morris!

The day before, Elisabeth had stolen the keys for the main entertaining room and had been making secret preparations. She had recruited additional helpers over the weekend and Johnny was hauled in as an extra pair of hands as well. All the usuals were there - Pendulum Brown, Mr. Potter, John Dunn, Colonel Kennard and many others from within the club. Horace Hutchinson and Charles Hutchins gave speeches and even Johnny, the man of few words, was happy to make his contribution. He had needed little persuasion to do so for his father. The evening was rounded off in good style by rousing, drunken singing conducted with typical, wild gusto by Mr. Owen Potter and accompanied by Pendulum Brown on the piano. Johnny's father had planned to get rid of the piano! It hadn't been touched for many months. He was glad he hadn't. It was played with feeling that evening.

The mess left over from the night's revelries seemed to take forever to clear up. Despite her hangover Elisabeth didn't mind. It was a small price to pay to see her father enjoying himself once more.

The party in John Ball Senior's honour was just the kick he needed. Within a few days he was back visiting the new clubhouse and playing golf with a passion that befitted a youngster.

Behind the scenes Johnny was the first to thank his sister for all she had done. It had taken a woman's touch to make it happen. It also made them both recognise that despite the construction of the new clubhouse, the friendships that had been forged over so many years were still there, as strong as ever. Significantly for Johnny's father, those friendships were still strongly linked with The Royal Hotel, where it had all started twenty six years previously.

Over the next few years it would be others who would steal the limelight on the golfing fairways. In 1896 Freddie Tait finally fulfilled the faith that so many Scots had put in him. Not only did he win the Amateur, he won it at St. George's, the venue that had strong English blood running through its core. Two years later he won again, this time at Hoylake. The night before the final the strains of his bagpipes could be heard piercing through the bars of The Royal Hotel and later in the centre of town in Market Street. He revelled in showing off his deep-seated Scottish heritage and would do all he could to summon up the spirits to help him stride forth into battle. It had clearly worked. His success would at least go some way to redressing the balance of English dominance in the game. Significantly he had also won on Johnny's home patch.

In the professional game, the picture for Scotland was bleaker. Following J.H. Taylor's back-to-back successes, Harry Vardon added salt to the wounds of the beleaguered Scots by winning the first of his many Opens. Scottish pride in their national game, the one they had invented was taking a damaging blow.

Golf was blossoming south of the border in England's green and pleasant land. In 1887 there were just fifty courses. Within fifteen years that total had risen to almost 1,000. Johnny's success had been in part responsible for this. He had been the strong resolute Englishman who had stood firm against all that had been thrown at him. He had ignited the passions of his countrymen and had raised the profile of the game in England, starting first in Hoylake and then spreading out to the more far-flung parts of the country. The subsequent success of others in the professional game, of Vardon and Taylor had added to the public desire to take up the game as a challenging and healthy pastime. Now landowners were starting to see that money could be made from investing in the building of courses and new housing stock that would surround them. The cost of labour for their construction was cheap, the profits to be gained potentially large. The growth of the railways was changing the face of urban living and was increasing the public's access to healthy sporting facilities.

Johnny's mantle had been taken up by others, by Harold Hilton, his junior stablemate, who would go on to win two Open Championships, and by the expertise of the English professionals. J.H. Taylor possessed the bulldog spirit that the crowds loved. He would bring golf to the masses by instigating the building of many public courses. He was a solidly built man with a strong never-say-die spirit. Vardon had Johnny's grace, his style and his technical ability. He also enjoyed the media attention and had the charisma and desire to spread the word that Johnny lacked. In time both Taylor and Vardon would take advantage of their successes by promoting the game through regular exhibition matches throughout the country. As professionals it was in their self-interest to do so. With additional financial backing they could earn considerable sums from the game. Johnny was an amateur, a farmer. He had no wish to be in the limelight, yet it followed him everywhere he went. He was quite happy to let others take centre stage and to reap the financial gains and plaudits from their endeavours.

# Tait and Ball Go Head to Head

By the time the Amateur Championship returned to Prestwick in 1899, Johnny had barely threatened in any of the major tournaments. Even on his home course where the Open had been staged at Hoylake for the very first time two years previously, he failed to make any real showing. His disappointing performance left the scene free for Hilton to take the limelight and walk away victorious. Again Johnny's supporters doubted whether he had the fight to bounce back and questioned whether his star had faded once and for all. Had it now been outshone, by another more youthful and more flamboyant one, by the younger Harold Hilton?

The spring of 1899 was, on the face of it, no different to any other. The winter had been a little colder, but all Johnny's cattle had survived and the calves were in good shape. His golf was slowly improving and he was beginning to find his form once more.

It was late afternoon after another win when Jack bumped into Johnny down by the hotel. Jack had needed a break from his workshop and had walked down to sit on one of the benches outside. It was good timing as he needed to have a quick word with his old friend.

'Hey Johnny. I've got a letter here. There's someone who wants to say hello.'

He waved the note paper in his direction.

'It's Tom, he wants to know whether you're going to make it up to Prestwick again this year for the Amateur. He can sort you out with some good digs and he'd love to catch up with you. I'll be writing back by the return post. What do you want me to say?'

'Tell him thanks and yes, I'd love to see him and if he could arrange for somewhere for me to stay, I'd be very grateful.'

Two months later and over one hundred hopefuls had turned out to compete in the last Amateur of the century. Johnny was amongst them. The field was almost three times that of when he had first won here eleven years previously. The local bars and hotels would be grateful for that.

Once play commenced, Johnny cruised through the early rounds but things proved far tighter in the quarter finals. He needed an extra hole to secure victory over an old foe, Robert Maxwell.

As was so often the case, these first few matches were proving just a warm up for Johnny. His opponent in the semis, G.C Wigham was dispatched with consummate ease. It left a final which everyone had hoped for. Freddie Tait, he of the Black Watch Regiment and the one who carried the hopes and prayers of all native Scots, would be Johnny's proud challenger.

Tait was in the form of his life, having won almost every competition he had entered in the last few months. He was also the current title holder and playing on home soil. Unsurprisingly, he was the firm favourite.

Reassuringly Johnny slept well that night. He might not have expected to, given the prospects of having to perform the following day, but he remained quite calm. Despite all the excitement such occasions never seemed to bother him.

Amongst the many goodwill messages he received before play began were those from his sister Elisabeth and from his good friend Tom. Tom had been especially generous in his words of encouragement. As Johnny prepared for his play the following day, the scene was much the same as ever in the accommodation he had rented: a table in the corner with a single candle flickering away, a bible perched on the side of his bed should he need it and his stylish golfing attire laid out on the chair opposite, all ready for the following day's contest. He could have been anywhere in the country but he was as prepared as ever. Tonight however he felt different. Tonight he felt calmer and more prepared for all that was to come. Within no time he fell into a deep sleep.

Whatever positive thoughts he might have had the previous evening they had little effect on his game the following day. Tait fairly stormed out of the blocks. He was five up by the 14th and although Johnny pulled his lead back to three by the half-way mark, the crowd sensed a home win was on the cards.

Back at Hoylake news had reached The Royal Hotel by telegram and the mood was glum. Elisabeth was instantly transported back to the previous summer and the sounds of those bagpipes that had drifted across the course from the clubhouse the night before the final. Freddie Tait had an aura about him which marked him out from the crowd. Johnny was battling this as much as the man himself.

'Come on Johnny,' she whispered to herself and gave the sideboard an extra firm polish as encouragement.

By the time the players made it through to the 6th hole, her resolve seemed to have worked. Had she added extra magic to the beeswax? Her brother had pulled it back to level. A win on the 13th and incredibly Johnny was one ahead. An updated telegram arrived and Elisabeth gave a quick skip round the furniture.

His play continued in its rich vein of good form and he remained one ahead by the time they played the 'Alps', their 17th. By this stage it seemed that the whole of Scotland had turned out to see them.

Lining every inch of the fairway, bodies scrambled in every direction, all eager for a clear sight of their man. Most surrounded the green as they awaited the arrival of Tait's ball. Few though, could see the man himself. His shot was blind, hidden by the towering dunes.

As the proud Scot picked his club, he hesitated. Turning to his caddie, he summoned him back to call for a replacement. A quick adjustment to his jacket and he settled in. The club went back smoothly enough but the follow through was ugly. He chunked it. Heavy overnight rain combined with a wet spring, had left many of the bunkers under water. The one in front of the 17th green was more like a lake and Tait had found it. It was greeted by audible groans from the crowd. Could Johnny take advantage? A win here and the title was his.

He had 140 yards to the green, for Johnny, a mashie. On approaching his ball he sent his caddie up ahead to give him the line over the dunes. He had played this shot at Prestwick many times before. Despite all that was at stake it held no fear for him but he still needed his caddie's direction.

The normal grace was there in his swing but in all his calculations he had forgotten one crucial factor – the force of the wind above the protection of the dunes. As the ball rose, it stalled. As it faltered, so the partisan applause increased. Pitching on the two foot bank in front of the green, his ball took one quick look, teetered momentarily on the edge before rolling slowly back into the wet sand at the front of the flooded bunker. The noise levels increased tenfold. Cat calls pierced the air. Scotland's hero was somehow still in the game, be it ankle deep.

It was Tait to play first. No relief here from a floating lie, he had no choice but to play the ball as he found it. The play was exquisite, the result remarkable - a splashed bunker shot to twenty feet[12]. More wild celebrations, but they had barely begun to subside before Johnny had likewise caressed his ball onto the sodden green ahead. Anything you can do...

The putts that followed were only likely to disappoint. Both took two to get down and Johnny remained one up with one to play. Few amongst the band of loyal English supporters will want to recall how Johnny let his opponent back in on the last but somehow he did and regretfully they moved to the first play-off hole.

---

[12] Exactly 100 years later Jean Van De Velde was faced with exactly the same prospect of playing from a floating lie in the Barry Burn at the final hole of The Open at Carnoustie. He declined the challenge on that occasion but at the time thousands criticised him for even considering it. Few though recognised that an almost identical shot had indeed been played by Freddie Tait all those years ago. What's more he had executed it, almost to perfection.

Sensing a Scottish win, the stewards struggled to silence the crowds as Johnny teed off. Yet again he was through his shot before many looked up. It proved the perfect antidote to the constant jibes and the taunts. For once, he outstripped his adversary by more than twenty yards and was now in the driving seat. He played his second to just eight feet. Tait had gone before him but had left himself a tricky twenty footer.

Not even the will of a thousand Scots could coax Tait's putt the final few inches he needed. He came up just short. All the time in the background, Johnny prowled, stalking his putt, checking the line from every angle. He signalled to Tait to remove his ball. His two inch putt was conceded. The focus was now on Johnny. Could he fight the will of the wild, unruly Scots? Johnny's confidence in his putting had been poor all week, to the point where he had been using a simple straight-faced iron to putt with. He needed it to perform for him now like never before. No quiet, respectful silence accompanied his stroke. With nerves of steel he stroked it clean and true and the cup rattled to the sound of victory against all odds.

With his win he had stolen Scotland's beating heart. He had done so at the very heart of the nation's living game. Freddie Tait immortalised the Gaelic spirit - the handsome bagpipe player, the rugged member of the Black Watch now slain by English blood on Scottish soil. Not quite Culloden but history had been made. Tait had taken the crown at Hoylake the previous year. Johnny had won it back again from under their very noses.

Bernard Darwin, the respected writer described his win as, 'the greatest, the most prostratingly exciting of them all'.

Tait was magnanimous and courteous to the end. In his presentation speech he would state that, 'I would rather be beaten by Johnny Ball than by any other man in the world.'

Back in Hoylake the news broke late. 'Ball wins at 37th Hole.'

Cue the celebrations. Jack poured himself a double whisky, Elisabeth grabbed her father and danced round the room. The real celebrations began a few days later, but not before Johnny was met with wild acclaim on his return to Hoylake station. A carriage pulled by 'human horses' whisked him home and the songs and merriment went on until dawn. Johnny was King of the Links once more.

With all the celebrations Johnny hadn't yet unpacked. For too long he had been at the beck and call of all those around him; of those who had been so keen to offer him their heartfelt congratulations. He had been longing to get away from the clamour, from the crowds and the adulation. For the first time in two days he finally had a few moments to himself. His bag was heavy; the contents filled with woollen tweed jackets, hobnail boots, waistcoats and linen shirts – all the garments required for play out on the links. As he unbuckled the leather straps of his case and lifted back the lid, the strong, pungent smell of sweat soaked clothes filled the air. He tucked the culprits away in the corner and opened a window. He wouldn't be getting much sleep with those damp clothes around him. The half empty case still contained his wash bag, his cap and tucked in the corner, a small envelope. He picked it up and took it over to the candlelight. He was puzzled. Where had it come from and how had he missed it when he was packing? It was only small, just normal letter size. His name was neatly written in black ink on the front. Whoever had done it had sneaked it into his bag before he left. With a strained, quizzical look he carefully opened one side. The contents revealed a brief note. It read simply,

'Remember you have Young Tom's spirit with you. Play well Johnny and good luck, Jack.'

He slumped back in the chair behind him. That overwhelming feeling of calm that had come over him as he fell asleep the night before, that final hole, that final putt.... Maybe Jack was right.

# The Boer War

For the past three years Johnny had been training as a reservist with the Denbighshire Yeomanry. He had volunteered with his good friend Ted Savage. No-one expected that it would lead any further, least of all Johnny himself, but a few months after his win at Prestwick, his commitment would be tested to the full.

Tension had been building in South Africa ever since the government's attempt to overthrow President Kruger's Transvaal Government in 1896. Britain was desperately trying to hold on to the last vestiges of her empire and she felt the need to stand up for what she felt was rightfully hers. At home the national fervour remained strong. Nothing exemplified the British spirit more than the patriotism evoked by composers such as Edward Elgar, who would later be knighted for his services to music. In the summer of 1899 he would conduct his first performance of The Enigma Variations, a piece of work for which he would forever be remembered. It typified the mood of the nation.

Britain was keen to establish a strong foothold across South Africa where her interest had been fuelled by the discovery of precious minerals. Dissent from the local Boers reached a tipping point when war was finally declared in October 1899. Back home the call went out for men to sign up. Johnny now had a decision to make but he was under no obligation to commit himself. As a volunteer, he didn't have to accept the King's shilling. British forces would enlist thousands from all parts of the United Kingdom to support the South African campaign. In Edinburgh, a certain Lieutenant Tait had received his orders from his command superiors. It was standard practice and he took the news in his stride. He always expected that one day he might be called up to the front line, after all this was his profession. Within a couple of weeks he would be heading south on board the Orient bound for Cape Town.

Johnny, on the other hand, had a choice. He was only a volunteer but he fervently believed in his country. He had farmed the land to help feed his fellow countrymen. He was a fit, highly skilled horseman and a fine shot, skills that were desperately needed. In the end his commitment would match that of Ted's. They had made up their minds. They would join up together.

In Freddie Tait and Johnny Ball you couldn't find more single-minded men. They may have been opponents a few months earlier, fighting head to head for a sporting crown, but now they were together as one, fighting a far more real and common enemy.

Johnny was nothing if not resolute, but it emphasised how little people knew of this modest, unassuming man that he had decided to enlist. He, like Tait was patriotic to the core, determined in the extreme.

For Johnny's father there were still significant practicalities to sort out. John Ball Senior was advancing in years and he still had a busy hotel to run. Reinforcements would certainly be required. He would need extra support from his daughters and another pair of hands behind the bar in the evening.

Unlike her father Elisabeth was more taken aback by the news. As a loving sister she was deeply concerned that she might never see her brother again. However she knew better than to try and dissuade him from going. It would have done little good in any case. She was briefly put out that he hadn't confided in her privately but then she understood his commitment to the cause. His was a personal decision which she had to respect.

Elisabeth had little chance of spending any valuable time with her brother in the weeks preceding his departure due to his training commitments in Aldershot. The only way in which she could readily express her feelings and let him know what he truly meant to her was by putting pen to paper. Johnny received her letter just a few days before his departure.

'Dear Johnny

*I want you to know how proud I am of you for having chosen to sign up. I also know that you will not have made this decision lightly. Our forces are extremely lucky to have a man who is so highly skilled, so brave and immensely able in every way.*

*It goes without saying that this letter is sent with every love from your devoted sister who will be praying every night for your safe return.*

*Godspeed Johnny.*

*All my love,*

*Elisabeth'*

It was a touching letter, short and to the point. Throughout the campaign Johnny kept it close and never let it leave his side.

From the time he enlisted to the date he set sail for South Africa it would be a mere three months.

At The Royal Liverpool Golf Club, members found other ways of marking their appreciation of the sacrifice Johnny was making. They also wanted to recognise his achievement of winning the Amateur Championship for a record fifth time. An incredible sum of £300 was raised to pay for his portrait to be painted by the artist Mr R. E. Morrison and it still hangs in the clubhouse to this day. He was showered with gifts, some eminently practical, others not. He was presented with a gold-crested watch and chain, a pistol and some field glasses. By far the most precious gift was a war horse, or by its rightful name, a charger, an extremely unusual gift but one which touched him deeply. It took much effort to train him, (when time eventually permitted Johnny to do so), and he would prove a faithful servant to him during his time at the front.

When the hour came to leave Hoylake, his send-off was akin to those he had experienced so often before after his successes on the fairways across Britain. This time however, the circumstances were entirely different. With hundreds gathered at the station and crowds cheering, his train finally departed accompanied by fog signals exploding in every direction. The explosions he would experience in the months to come would sadly be of a very different nature.

Almost three weeks after setting sail, Johnny arrived tired and exhausted at Durban. His regiment was given its orders and he was moved up towards the front line.

He was forced to endure some fierce fighting during the campaign. Within a few months he would sustain some minor injuries to his legs but he would soon return to the front after treatment. When fighting became more intense reports suggested that his courage in the face of heavy fire was unfailing.

The troop had been given warning that by daybreak they would advance on the enemy through the small gap in the breakwater to the left of their current position. When the order to advance was given one man was brought down and his charger fell pinning him down, leaving him exposed to enemy crossfire. Johnny was the first to his rescue and with little or no concern for his own wellbeing got the flailing horse up from the wretched man's legs. Bullets were flying in every direction. He pulled the man free. It was a display of immense courage and bravery. He would admit to none of his actions afterwards but the events had been witnessed by his very own colleagues. He had gone well beyond the call of duty.

Johnny wrote home to his sister on a regular basis. She treasured the letters he sent and would read them over and over before replying with words of love and encouragement.

For fear of worrying her he was generally sparse with the truth and the horrors that he witnessed, but on one occasion, even he couldn't hide the sadness he felt. He wrote of how after an especially fierce attack from the enemy, Ted was shot and later died of his injuries. Johnny was left the painful duty of sorting through his possessions and of helping to dig his final resting place.

'It was the hardest task I shall ever have to perform,' he wrote in his letter home to Elisabeth.

The closest Johnny came to death was evidenced by a scar that was left on his neck by a bullet which came within inches of ending his life. Sadly, the gods were not so kind to Scotland's golfing idol. After surviving a severe wounding in the early days of the conflict, Freddie Tait returned once again to the front line in January 1900. It was the final action he would face. On 7th February in the battle of Koodoosberg Drift, he was shot and fatally wounded, destined never to see his homeland again or to grace the fairways of the golfing world, where for a brief period, he had once been king. Scottish golf went into deep mourning. Their gallant hero had been mown down in his prime.

Johnny was only too relieved when in late June it was announced that his troop would be returning home. He longed for his home life and his farm. He would never speak of the events that he witnessed but inside he was deeply disturbed by all that he had experienced. A sketch that appeared in the local paper showed Johnny bravely astride his charger laying waste to an attacker with his sword accompanied by the words 'Laying him dead on the green'. It was an entirely inappropriate and jingoistic comparison between his brave actions in battle and his bold play on the golf course. The two worlds could not have been further apart. It was recognition, if needed, that few understood the true nature of war.

The celebrations laid on for his homecoming were in his view totally unwarranted. The townsfolk of Hoylake and indeed his own family saw things very differently. In their eyes Johnny had played a key part in defending the nation's honour and he deserved all the thanks and adulation that was heaped upon him. Within days he was back out in the fields working on his farm.

# Back on Home Soil

In Johnny's absence his father had kept a watchful eye on the farm and had ensured that the wages for his two labourers, Joe and Dan were paid. However it was Jack who had been good enough to take on overall responsibility for the day-to-day management of the farm and for the supervision of the two lads. Johnny's father was sadly becoming increasingly frail and it was enough for him to keep the hotel going with the continued support of his daughters and his two other paid staff.

Johnny had just finished the milking when a familiar face appeared from around the parlour door.

'Anyone home?' came the cry.

'In here, come on through.'

Jack turned the corner to find Johnny scrubbing down over a sink.

'How does it feel to be back?' Jack asked.

'Good.'

If there was anything more to be added to Johnny's one word response he wasn't going to say it. He wouldn't let on to anyone how he felt about his time away.

'Hey, you could have fixed the leak at the back of the barn in the far paddock for me,' Johnny called out as he dried his hands in the corner. 'Water's streaming down the side there.'

Jack was taken aback. He couldn't recall any signs of a leak in that barn. He could have sworn the buildings were in good order. He had checked them the day before Johnny returned.

A grin spread over Johnny's face as he looked back over to Jack sitting at the table. And then he clicked. Johnny was pulling his leg. There was no leak. It was his roundabout way of thanking him for all he had done whilst he was away. Johnny took great pride in the upkeep of his farm and as the caretaker whilst he was away, Jack had passed the test with flying colours.

Johnny always knew that the running of his smallholding would be in safe hands. Jack's enthusiasm and practical skills in managing a links were enough to ensure the farm continued to thrive in his absence.

Many years had passed since the early days when Jack had shepherded Johnny round Scotland's renowned links and had offered him words of support and encouragement. Their friendship ran deep and whilst Johnny may have been a man of few words, a brief look between the two of them was enough to reinforce the bond that had been sealed all those years ago.

Both had moved on since those early days and each had gained prestige in their own right, not that either of them saw it that way. Jack had won considerable respect from the many Club Secretaries and members who had passed through during his time at Hoylake. He had taught several hundred over the years, many of them rich and famous, but he had always maintained the same charm and encouraging demeanour from which so many had benefited. His status within the club and the town was firmly established even if his annual retainer of £20 didn't truly reflect it. Johnny's standing had risen a hundredfold since winning his first boy's medal back in 1872. His haul of five Amateur titles, an Open Championship, three Irish titles and countless club gold medals was truly impressive. On top of this he could now add a bravely fought campaign in South Africa to his achievements. His star could hardly have shone brighter.

Whilst he had been away on the battlefields of South Africa, a 30 year old Harold Hilton had been keeping his adversaries at bay on the far friendlier fields and fairways closer to home. He had won the 1900 Amateur Championship at St. George's in Kent and had done so in style by the considerable margin of 8 and 7 against James Robb of Scotland in the final. It was his first success in the competition having come so close many times before. Harold had stolen a jewel from Johnny's crown. Elisabeth knew this only too well, for although such things didn't trouble Johnny, she was keen that her brother should still prove himself as the best amongst the amateurs. By late spring however, she had become concerned. She had heard neither sight nor sound of her brother. The upper floors of the tall, three-storey hotel provided an ideal vantage point and the characteristic silhouette of the champion golfer out in the sand hills had been missing for a couple of months. During an afternoon break she headed over to the farm.

As she turned the corner into the farmyard she heard an audible yelp from one of the barns.

Johnny was sitting on a bench holding his hand which was half-bound by some tired-looking strapping.

'This damned wrist. Those cobs, they've got a mind of their own. I couldn't hold them back. That's the second time they've pulled away like that with no warning.'

Elisabeth sat down next to him and carefully unwrapped the strapping.

'It's badly swollen, Johnny and what's that scar there? That looks nasty.'

'Oh it's nothing. Something I picked up…'

Johnny hesitated. He was struggling for words. For a brief moment they looked at one another in silence. The scar was a good four inches long. It had healed well but there was little doubt where it had come from. Johnny sat up straighter and shifted to a more comfortable position. Elisabeth took the hint and moved away. It was clear that Johnny had nothing more to say on the matter.

'Stay there a moment. Have you got anything stronger or firmer we could use to strap it up with?'

'Try one of the drawers in the kitchen. There's some old cloth in there. That might do.'

Elisabeth made her way next door and returned with the cloth. Slowly, carefully she wound the cloth over and round, over and round until it formed a firmer support to the injured hand.

'Is there much more you need to do today?'

'Only the milking and the fences that need repairing at the back and the…. '

'All right, all right. I understand but can't one of the lads do that for you?'

Elisabeth felt the sense of frustration in Johnny's tone.

'I suppose so.'

'Where are they now?'

'They're having a break.'

'Well, I'll have a word with them when they get back.'

Elisabeth was taking charge. It seemed only natural, instinctive. She had shown similar care for her grandfather in the last years of his life, but the desire to take over and care for her younger brother was even stronger. Beyond the tough exterior there was a vulnerability in Johnny that went well beyond any physical scar, one which his sister would do anything to protect.

Golf was out of the question for the next two months. Despite help from his farmhands many of the jobs that Johnny needed doing would have to wait. He was hopeless at delegating. Nobody could match his high standards. He was a perfectionist and that was that.

~

The turn of the century was a defining time for the club and the country. Queen Victoria's death in 1901 marked the end of an era and brought with it a sense of apprehension in the public's mind as to the future of the nation and the empire as a whole. The Boer War was still being fought but the final Treaty of Vereeniging would soon be signed. It would prove a significant step towards South African independence.

There were no signs of instability within The Royal Liverpool Golf Club. The club had decided to appoint a new and forward-thinking Secretary by the name of Harold Janion and he took little time in reinforcing the club's standings at the top table of golf. The year of 1902 saw the club host not only the Amateur Championship but the Open Championship as well. As if this wasn't enough, Janion had gone one stage further and had been bold enough to inaugurate a brand new Amateur competition between the world's two leading golf nations, Scotland and England. For years, debate had raged as to who held supremacy in the game. A team match might settle things once and for all. In any case Janion had no wish to see another club organise a match which so many felt was long overdue. Johnny had been involved in countless fierce contests between the two countries and more recently Harry Vardon and J.H. Taylor had stamped their authority on the professional game for England. Between Vardon, Taylor and Hilton, no Scot would get a look-in between 1894 and 1900 in the Open Championship, but these were individual wins. What of a team contest?

As the new century dawned, Vardon would be astute enough to take advantage of his success by persuading the American based Spalding Company to back him on a major tour of the States. It would see him stage over 90 challenge and exhibition matches in just nine months. He would remain unbeaten throughout his tour which would reach its climax at the United States Open Championship in Chicago. He would sweep all aside here as well, returning across the pond in 1900 with the trophy firmly in his grasp. For the present, England reigned supreme in the world of professional golf and by the evidence of the last few years it wasn't doing too badly in the amateur stakes as well.

Many from both sides of the English and Scottish border now clamoured for the right to boast their nation as best in the world of golf. A team competition would prove once and for all who was top dog. Janion proposed that the match be staged the week before the Amateur

Championship and it was met with instant approval by the golfing elite from both sides of the border.

Much speculation took place as to how the outcome of the match would be judged. Would it be by the number of individual matches won on each side or by the total number of holes won, these being accumulated across all the matches. In the end the decision was made to go with the latter.

There were no surprises when the contestants' names were released. The two most famous schools of golf - St. Andrews and The Royal Liverpool Golf Club dominated proceedings. Ball, Hilton, Hutchings and Darwin were the first to be nailed to the English mast but surprisingly John Graham, a rising star who was a firm favourite amongst the Hoylake members, chose to represent Scotland by virtue of his parents' Scottish ancestry. From St. Andrews, the familiar names of Balfour-Melville, Ferguson, Low and Robb all represented Scotland.

On the day of the contest special trains were laid on from Liverpool to accommodate the sizeable crowds that attended. As ever it was the public that would have a significant part to play in the outcome of the matches. Johnny had been drawn against an old foe, Robert Maxwell. Maxwell had learnt his golf under the tutelage of Ben Sayers in Edinburgh and had already put his prowess to good use to Johnny's detriment, in the 1897 Amateur. A tall, confident and powerful hitter, his style was in marked contrast to Johnny's grace and elegance. However, Johnny would unleash a new secret weapon during the match, an experimental ball which had only just arrived from the States. Its name was 'The Haskell'. Its advantage came in the extra length that could be gained off the tee. Made from a wound rubber core, it responded well to the drier and firmer fairways of the links courses. Johnny now had a new string to his bow. Whereas Maxwell had raw power Johnny used the latest technology and he had the guile and finesse to put it to good use.

For one unlucky spectator the morning's play came too close for comfort. As Maxwell launched a wild and errant drive on the third, the cries of fore went unheeded by the unruly crowds and a young child, oblivious to proceedings, was stretchered away with blood pouring from his head. This would prove the first of several spectator casualties. It would take many years before safer, rope-lined fairways were introduced on a regular basis.

The match ultimately finished with a win for Johnny although the outcome was far closer than many anticipated. He would achieve victory by just one hole. However his countryman couldn't match his endeavours and surprisingly Hilton was soundly beaten in both his morning and afternoon rubbers. In the end Scotland came away comfortable winners by seven holes.

The disgruntled home support was keen for their men to seek quick revenge. The Amateur Championship to be staged in just a few days' time would prove the perfect chance for them to do so.

It is strange how fate can bring up repeats of clashes in major tournaments, for just a few days later Johnny would meet Maxwell again in the second round. This time Johnny wasn't so fortunate, disappointing his supporters in the process by losing on the 17th. Their consolation was to see another fellow Hoylake man take the spoils, a Mr. Charles

Hutchings. He would finally succeed after an epic encounter in the final. No mean achievement for a man of 53 years.

The Open Championship which took place just a month later would be remembered for the success of the Haskell ball which Johnny had recently trialled but it wouldn't be too far-fetched to say that Johnny himself played a key role in determining the ultimate winner of the Championship.

The day before the competition started Johnny ended up pairing with Sandy Herd for his first practice round and they would strike up a firm friendship. Herd was a likeable professional from St. Andrews who had learned his trade at the home of golf but had subsequently moved to the Yorkshire mill town of Huddersfield. As they played Herd soon noticed the additional length Johnny was getting with his drives. When he was shown the ball Johnny was using Herd was quick to ask if he could borrow one for the remaining few holes. He was so impressed that within a few moments of his finishing his round, he had purchased the last remaining Haskells from Jack in his shop. Herd would be glad of any slight advantage when he teed off the following day.

Johnny was disappointed by his performance in his first two rounds and with two 79's was well off the pace. Herd however remained within touching distance. He was just 4 behind Vardon, who was now ensconced as firm favourite up front. By chance Johnny and Herd had been paired together for the final day and this was to work in Herd's favour.

There are times when golf can be maddening in the extreme. Players can strike shots that astound one moment and yet they can fall apart the next. By the time Herd approached his final few holes he had taken the lead but his game had gone to pieces. Known as 'the greyhound' for his swift and sure play, Vardon was now on Herd's tail and was catching up fast. There are strict rules within the game of golf to stop any player giving advice to another. There was no suggestion any advice was given but it was the mark of the man that Herd should state in his autobiography that, 'Mr Ball was more desirous that I should win than he was himself,' and that, 'he gave me every encouragement that one man can give another.' Johnny had taken every opportunity to praise his partner in his play and had given him the confidence to get over the line. Herd would go on to hold things together on the 18th and finally clinch the title for Scotland. 'The greyhound' had left it too late to catch his man. Herd meanwhile, had found a friendship that would last for years to come.

~

In the spring of the following year, 1903, a decision was made that would change Johnny's future for good. Lord Stanley, the owner of much of the land thereabouts, announced that he would be terminating the lease on Stand Farm. He was proposing to build a number of houses bordering the course on Meols Drive and five would be built over the land that Johnny had farmed for much of his life. The housing boom had come to Hoylake and there was little that could be done about it. There was one consolation. Three paddocks would be made available for lease a quarter of a mile away, closer to the River Birkett, but Johnny's income would be seriously threatened.

Johnny soon sold off most of his cattle but he still kept a head of fifteen which he moved to his newly rented fields. Over the next few months he would slowly run the farm down. His working future would now be tied up in the hotel.

Johnny was grateful for a busy few months here. Three major competitions had kept the tills turning and his father in clover. John Ball Senior was pleased to see new life brought back to a hotel in which he had invested so much of his heart and soul. Out on the course his son had struggled this year but he had long memories of his previous successes and he would continue to dine out on Johnny's victories. It was these that had kept him going in recent years but his fight and inner fire had gone. John Ball Senior's health was deteriorating.

In the summer of 1904 he started to lose weight rapidly. As ever it was Elisabeth who had noticed it. One evening she found him gasping for breath on a stool behind the bar.

By the following morning the doctor had been called and had diagnosed a painful and enlarged swelling in his mouth. It was giving him significant pain and was affecting his breathing. He had developed a carcinoma of the tongue. The prognosis sadly wasn't good. It would mean major surgery. By the summer the cancer had spread to his neck.

On the night of 16th July the doctor was summoned for the very last time. With Johnny and his family by his side, John Ball Senior passed away peacefully in his sleep.

The funeral was one of the largest Hoylake had ever known. Play at The Royal Liverpool Golf Club was suspended for the weekend and the club's flag lowered to half-mast in reverence to a man who had served the club so well. A guard of honour made up of club members greeted the coffin as it was raised on shoulders on arrival at Trinity Church in Hoylake. Johnny was one of the main pallbearers as he carried his father between the rows of golfers from England and Scotland who saluted the coffin with golf clubs raised. The church was barely big enough to accommodate the numbers who visited to pay their respects.

All were invited back to The Royal Hotel after the service and the chatter was loud and long. Elisabeth had booked caterers to feed the guests and she was meticulous in ensuring that all who attended received food and service to the standard that her father would have wanted. Johnny was proud to say a few simple words before the evening was over. It was a long, tiring day which passed as best it could.

During his lifetime John Ball Senior had had a huge impact on the town of Hoylake. He had been present at the birth of The Royal Liverpool Golf Club. Without his offer to rent out rooms at The Royal Hotel, the club would never have become established. He enabled the club to breath, to expand and to develop a life and personality of its own. He supported the members by providing entertainment in the form of bars, club meeting rooms and hotel space where golfers could relax and lay their weary heads both before and after their battles on the course. In time the club moved on and with reluctance he accepted the need for change but he was still able to offer the accommodation that travelling golfers needed. He had put Hoylake on the map, helping to transform it from a quiet fishing village to a seaside resort renowned for its golf, its waters and clean sea air.

The day after the funeral, it seemed that time had slowed to a crawl. An air of gloom had descended on the hotel. It was almost as if the very life, its heartbeat had been sucked out from within.

When Johnny woke the following morning his mind went back to his childhood years, to the time when his father would be calling out orders, serving his ale with proud bonhomie in packed bars with contented customers. In those days he had been keen to remain hidden from his parents for fear of engaging his father's wrath. Oh how he wished he might hear that booming, cutting voice once more. John Ball Senior had been a strict but fair man, proud of his son; a real father at a time when he himself had seen no great worth in his golfing achievements. John Ball Senior had built a thriving, bustling hotel which was valued and respected throughout Wirral. It would be left to Johnny and his sisters now to take that on. How they would do so, they didn't yet know but they would work it out between them in the weeks to come. For the moment Johnny needed time; time to come to terms with the fact that he was now the sole male and head of the family. The expectations were great.

It was early in the morning. No one had yet stirred and the remains from the wake were still scattered before him as Johnny came down the stairs into the bar. The pungent smells of stale beer filled the room and a smoky haze hung over the leather chairs and the solid wooden tables. Over by the main door the grandfather clock struck the hour of 7am. He grabbed the keys from under the bar and moved over to the front door. The turn of metal in the lock was louder, harsher than normal but the silence outside was gladly reassuring and peaceful. He looked out across the links; not a soul around at this time of day. His legs had a mind of their own and seemed to pull him seawards. He turned right down towards the shore where he could just make out the faint outline of Hilbre Island in the mist surrounded by a calm, innocent sea. The tide was at its highest this morning and the birds, pushed to the water's edge, were scurrying back and forth, probing, searching, eking out an existence in an untamed world. High above him, a skein of geese arrowed overhead, calling to one another as they went, urging their friends on to pastures new. Where will life take me now, Johnny wondered?

He had witnessed such a cruel and barbaric world on the plains and in the mountains of South Africa. Somehow he had got through that. He had returned and thrown himself into life back home, into his golf and his farm. Everything had moved on but this felt different. This was a loss, oh so personal, so much closer to home. It hit at who he was, who he had become and where he might go next. What was this all about – life, death, winning, losing, furthering oneself, making a journey like the geese and the oystercatchers on the ebb and flow of the tide? He yearned for peace in this time of turmoil, yet he was struggling to find it.

Over the next few days the trail of visitors was almost endless as they called to pass on their condolences to Johnny and his sisters. The siblings were grateful for the kind words which helped to reassure them of how much their father meant to so many at the club. His sisters felt the loss far more than Johnny. They had tended to their father, night and day over his final few weeks. They had ensured that he suffered as little as possible but they had given so much of themselves in the process. They were empty, almost incapable of putting even one foot in front of the other. They rattled around in a hotel that echoed of times gone by but suggested nothing of what was to come.

Despite it all life had to move on. There were fundamental decisions that needed to be made. What was to become of The Royal? Who would run it and how? It was a profitable hotel and a valuable asset but it needed managing.

The family's discussions regarding the hotel's future were long and drawn out. In the end it was decided that Johnny and his sisters would manage it between them. They were loath to appoint someone to act as manager in these, the early days after their father's death. They couldn't face the emotion of relinquishing immediate control of a business that he had built up so successfully over the years. It just felt the right thing to do. Strong communication and organisation would be required to make it work but they were used to that.

Over the next year or so Johnny just went through the motions on the links. He played and indeed won many of the club competitions he entered, including amongst others, the Lubbock and Kennard Gold medals and the Dowie Cup. He was even victorious away from home as well at Leasowe and Lytham. Remarkably he was still able to function automatically and defeat his nearest challengers by significant margins but his heart was never fully into his play. He continued to earn praise and yet he wanted it even less than before. He had become numb to it all. It was as if golf was what he did and he did it because it was harder not to. His biggest pleasure now came from spending time with Elisabeth but strangely not on the farm or away from the hotel. It was on the links. His sister had finally succumbed to the game that had surrounded her all her life and she had begun to excel at it. Over a two-day tournament at nearby Moreton the two progressed through round after round of foursomes play to be defeated only in the semi-finals by the eventual winners. They had made an agreement before they entered – no coaching, no apologies for poor play. They played together as one and were able to share a special time when each needed the support of the other more than ever. Ironically, at the end their pact was broken by none other than Johnny himself. It was he who missed the final crucial putt and ended up making the apologies to his sister.

By the time the Amateur returned to St. Andrews in 1907 Johnny's mind was more settled and more tuned in to the world which had seemed to have passed him by over the last year.

# St. Andrews and a Tribute to the Old Man of Golf

St. Andrews had never been Johnny's favourite course but he had strong reasons for going back. He was keen to erase the bad memories and his disastrous finish here in '95'.

Jack, his mentor of so many years and his most ardent supporter, was willing him to make the trip but he needed little persuasion. Both knew that with age creeping up on him, this might be his final chance of succeeding at this most hallowed of venues. Winning here would establish him as a true great in the eyes of those who counted. Overcoming the record field of two hundred would be a major achievement in itself.

By now there had developed a somewhat rebellious streak in Johnny. He had never been one to easily conform to the norms and general expectations of the day and as the years passed by he was keen to do things his own way and in his own unique style. A few months earlier he had bought himself a motorbike and he now revelled in the freedom of the open road. Having tested it out at home he decided to travel up to Scotland in style on his bike. Jack would take his clubs and would meet him there when he arrived. To add to his rebelliousness, just a few days before he left, Johnny took a razor to his moustache and shaved it off. For those around him he now appeared a totally different man. By the time he reached St. Andrews many thought that an entirely new golfer had arrived in their midst.

Johnny could have drawn any one of those two hundred competitors in the first round but somehow his name would be drawn against a past adversary who knew his game better than any other. A match between Johnny Ball and Johnny Laidlay seemed like a fixture that had been around since time began. Their previous battles had been long and hard fought. This contest would prove no different. The crowds were rubbing their hands at the prospects of yet another top level Scotland versus England encounter. They weren't to be disappointed. The play they witnessed would match some of the finest ever seen on this hallowed turf. Back and forth the momentum swung until the scores were still tied by the time the players came to the 17th. Each had matched the other, blow for blow; each had excelled beyond every expectation. Johnny would finally come out triumphant but it would take every ounce of his energy to get over the line.

This epic encounter seemed to concentrate Johnny's mind. He swept through the next few rounds and in the process was able to benefit from the unlikely scenario of seeing his biggest challengers fall by the wayside on the other side of the draw. He was soon through to the semi-finals to play a relatively unknown challenger in the form of Guy Campbell. Another Scot, Campbell would prove a tougher prospect. He would take the lead in the early stages but like so many others before him, would find Johnny's pace just too hot to handle. It would take a superb second shot to within two feet of the flag on the 16th, a trademark John Ball cleek, to finally clinch the match for the five time champion. It would see him through to his second St. Andrews final.

If the weather had been soft on the players until now, it bared its teeth for the final. A fierce north-westerly gale, laden with rain, lashed down on the players and the hardy, 2,000 strong crowd. It would test their every sinew, every muscle, leaving hands frozen to the bone and bodies drenched to the core. In any normal club competition players would never have ventured forth from the safety and protection of their snug clubhouses but this was the final. This was the pinnacle of amateur golf where players should be stretched to the limit. It was part of the game. This would be a test of will, of raw strength and of inner resolve.

The smart money was on Johnny. He was the man with the track record of holding firm and delivering when the chips were down. Few would back his challenger, C. A. Palmer, on a day like today. The unlikely finalist could not have faced a more determined opponent in any tougher conditions.

Unsurprisingly, the standard of play was poor. It was a case of survival and carry on regardless. There were bound to be casualties. Spectators saw umbrellas ripped from their grasp, hats tossed to the winds. Johnny himself would not go unscathed. A poor lie on the 3rd had given him no option but to dig his ball out. In the process his wrist took a sickening blow. His pain would only increase as he struggled for warmth and protection from the elements. Every blow caused him greater distress. He gritted his teeth and said not a word. His opponent was none the wiser but he had his own troubles to deal with. Johnny was standing firm. Palmer was falling further and further behind. By the 13th he was four down. By the halfway stage he had reduced the deficit to two but he would be grateful of the mid-way break for lunch.

Over a well-earned rest the players took the chance to dry out, warm up and change into fresh attire but if anything the conditions got worse. Jack and Tom gave up trying to follow in the vile weather and wisely stayed inside by the roaring fire. The old master of the greens may have been born of tough St. Andrean stock but he knew what was best for him today. Neither doubted who would prevail. Save for an ugly seven at the 4th Johnny parred his way home. Palmer's fate was finally sealed on the 14th. As he turned to shake the hand of the worthy winner his sunken eyes told the story of a man defeated not only by his opponent but by the elements as well.

After so many failed attempts Johnny had finally prevailed at St.Andrews, at the cradle of golf. On winning, Johnny anticipated the reception he would likely receive. He ran for cover but was cut off by his supporters and raised high in celebration on shoulders jubilant and strong. Tom and Jack were absent on the 14th green but would never have missed the final ceremony for the world. The trophy was presented to a man who would be welcomed into Scottish hearts. Soon after, Johnny was awarded honorary membership of the Royal and Ancient Golf Club, a rare and special privilege. It was given in recognition of him as a man as much as for his achievements in golf. He would be the first golfer ever to be given this accolade.

If winning at the home of golf wasn't enough there would be another reason for Johnny to feel glad he had competed but it was one that wouldn't become clear until many months later. Less than a year after that final putt was sunk came news that stunned the golfing world. Tom Morris, the father of the game, the high priest of all of golf, had died. A stumble at the top of the stairs in the New Golf Club adjacent to the St. Andrews' 18th fairway was enough for the 89 year old to trip and fall. After hitting his head on the stone steps he would never recover consciousness. The old man of golf had passed away. The golfing community took a massive intake of breath and wondered where next for the game.

No one could ever come close to matching Tom Morris' influence in the sport. He pioneered new approaches to green-keeping and as keeper of the greens of the two most prominent clubs in the world at the time, had introduced standards in upkeep and design that would revolutionise golf worldwide. He had crafted clubs and balls and had introduced the 'Guttie', a vast improvement to the feathery which had frustrated so many. He had lived the game, had breathed it all his life. He had won four Open Championships and had played in The Open consistently from its very beginning until the ripe old age of 75. His son, Young Tom, Johnny's boyhood hero, had been rightly acclaimed as the greatest golfer to have lived and had partnered his father to win many outstanding foursome challenge matches. Above all Tom was respected and liked by all from every class, every background.

For Johnny, Tom was his grandfather figure. He had appeared from nowhere at many of his championships, sending smoke signals of delight from his trusty old pipe, nodding his approval to so much that Johnny had done. He had admired Johnny's modest approach to the game. They saw eye to eye on so many aspects of golf course design. Tom was a traditionalist and yet saw the need for the game to move on. Could it have been that it was through Tom's influence at the Royal and Ancient that Johnny had received his honorary membership?

Tom's funeral was the biggest ever seen in the city of St. Andrews. In the short space of time when his coffin was taken from his home, through the cobbled streets of the city, along South Street to the ruins of the old Cathedral, people stood in silent tribute. Not a soul turned in to work. Every man, woman and child came out to line the streets and to see St. Andrews' greatest servant pass by for the final time. Jack and George acted as proud pallbearers as Tom's coffin was finally laid to rest in the family grave. It was their saddest hour and a sad time for the golfing world.

It took a long time for golf to recover from the events of August 1908 but move on it did. Although Tom could never be replaced, his legacy would live on through the courses he designed and the passion and enthusiasm he instilled in so many.

# Summoning up the Hoylake Gods

By 1907 Annaud Massy had raised the standard for France by winning the Open Championship at Hoylake. It was a unique achievement for a man who represented a nation that had never before come close to winning at this the highest level of golf. The Frenchman's success was an indication of how the game had spread. His pride in his win was revealed when he would later christen his daughter 'Hoylake', in celebration of his victory there. His win would also come at a time when a tall and likeable Scot in the form of James Braid would make his mark on the game by winning the Open Championship an incredible five times in just ten years. Alongside Taylor and Vardon, Braid would go on to form part of the irrepressible 'triumvirate of golf' that would dominate the professional game for a twenty year period leading up to the outbreak of the First World War.

In the amateur game, Robert Maxwell, the Scot with whom Johnny had tussled on more than a few occasions, finally took the title in 1909 to leave the Scots dominant once more in both the professional and amateur games.

When the Amateur Championship returned to Hoylake in 1910, it was a chance for Johnny to redress the balance in England's favour but with fresh talent on the scene, he would need to raise his game to do so.

Johnny progressed relatively smoothly in the first few rounds, but came up against far stiffer opposition in the form of J.B. Pease in the fourth. He needed to be at his very best to overcome his opponent's splendid opening thirty six shots for the first 9 holes. Only four consecutive 3's after the turn were sufficient for him to finally win on the 16th. Next up was an equally tough opponent in F.W. Weaver. Again Johnny prevailed, but he was taken all the way to the 18th in doing so.

His opponent in the quarter-final was Robert Harris, a successful Scottish-born golfer who now worked at the London Stock Exchange. A bold player twenty years Johnny's junior, he got off to a flying start, winning the first three holes. Once more Johnny pulled it back. By the 13th he was level again. Both players would par in from here to take the game down the 19th. Time had now come for the Hoylake weather to play its part. It left the valiant golfers acting out the final scene with their coat tails thrashing round their waists in the wild, swirling wind. Barely able to stand as they teed off outside the clubhouse, somehow they carried on. As they prepared to play their second shots, there was nothing in it. Both balls now lay side by side at the corner of the raised turf cop. Harris was up first and clipped his ball pure and sweet. The green was his and for a moment he felt the game was won. Not so. His opponent was majestic in response and likewise found the short turf 170 yards ahead. With Johnny holing out in a further two putts and Harris putting up to four feet for his next, the Scot needed one last putt to half the match.

It was at this point that Hoylake seemed to take care of its own. As Harris took his putter back, so the thunder rolled. As if the script had already been written, his ball swung agonisingly wide. Johnny was through to the semi-final and Hoylake's weather gods had claimed another victim.

Logic would suggest that as the rounds progressed, so the matches should get harder, but golf has never been a logical game. Johnny easily disposed of Abe Mitchell in the semis to book a place in his 9th Amateur final. He would be playing C.C. Aylmer, the Secretary of the Strathpfeffer Golf Club, near Dingwall in Scotland.

On the morning of the final Johnny rose early but he had played in many such matches and knew what to expect – the crowds, the cheering, the highs and the lows. He was used to the many ups and downs that match play[13] golf can bring. The contest was a marathon, not a sprint. His time on the battlefields and his work out on the fields of his farm had given him the strength and the fortitude to cope with whatever was thrown his way. As a man who had survived the atrocities of war there was little that truly fazed John Ball.

It was only 6am and all around was calm and still in The Royal Hotel but Johnny had one small duty to perform. He grabbed a small bag of corn and went through to the courtyard at the back of the hotel. He had some little friends who needed his attention. His chickens needed feeding. They would produce the eggs to be served up to his hotel guests during their stay. With a bit of luck they would have already laid a clutch for him to take through to the breakfast table before he teed off. With a sweep of the hand, he

---

[13] Match play golf, as the term suggests is a one on one competition against your opponent where the result is decided on the number of holes won. All Amateur Championships are played under match play conditions.

scattered the seed onto the gravel. He had been doing this all his life, bringing nourishment to the soil, food to the table, satisfaction to his soul. Sure enough there they were; half a dozen eggs, still warm, all ready for serving in a few hours time.

Play finally got under way at 10am and Johnny was imperious throughout. Aylmer would never get a look in. By the 9th hole of the second round the players shook hands and the plaudits rang out once more for Johnny Ball. The local favourite was champion for the seventh time, and for the third and final time at his home course here at Hoylake. Everyone celebrated and even the chickens were pleased. They produced twice the number of eggs by the following morning.

The next year would prove a notable one for both Hoylake and for the nation. The public was in joyous mood following the coronation of King George V and the event was marked locally by the pealing of the bells at the opening of Liverpool's iconic new masterpiece, The Royal Liver Building. In the world of golf it was Hoylake's own who would walk off with the Amateur title at Prestwick. This time it would be Hilton who would prevail and he would follow his victory with further success in the United States by winning the US Amateur Championship. A British player had never won both amateur titles in the same year. Few had ever tried. It was a magnificent achievement. Johnny had a serious rival once more and he needed to do something about it.

# The Final Hurrah

There was little doubt that England was riding high in the game. Hilton had been successful both at home and in the States and Johnny had won the amateur prize the year before. The Scots were nowhere to be seen. The signs didn't look good for them again when the venue for the 1912 Amateur was announced. It would be held in a corner of England that few even knew existed - in the furthest reaches of north east Devon, at Westward Ho.

The Royal North Devon Club or 'Westward Ho', as it was more commonly known, was England's oldest links course. Established in 1864 just five years before The Royal Liverpool Golf Club, it could easily rival the best courses in Scotland in terms of its quality but it had always suffered from its remote location. Unsurprisingly, the numbers who turned up to compete were considerably lower than normal – just 134 in total.

The course had risen to prominence largely through the recent success of its most famous son, J.H. Taylor. Taylor had started here as a caddie and within a few years had moved on to the position of resident professional. He would subsequently go on to compete on the national stage and in time would win five Open Championship titles. On the amateur side, one of its early members, Horace Hutchinson, had likewise been successful, winning the Amateur Championship twice and coming runner-up on a further two occasions. He had also firmly established himself as a prolific writer and respected figure in the game. Thus the course had strong credentials and was more than worthy of hosting the most celebrated of all amateur tournaments.

The Championship was due to take place at the end of April. In normal circumstances it would have been front page news in any of the sporting papers but an event had taken place just a few days before its start that would shock the world. The HMS Titanic, the flagship of the White Star Line and the largest trans-Atlantic liner ever to be built, had struck an iceberg on its maiden voyage and had sunk with the loss of over 1,500 lives. The world had witnessed nothing like it, a disaster on an unprecedented scale. It was with sombre hearts that many golfers stepped up to the first tee after a minute's silence on the morning of 25th April 1912.

Only six rounds were needed to make the final but having comfortably made it through to the quarters Johnny's hopes of getting there seemed doomed. He had been drawn against a relative novice in F.S. Bond. Novice or not, Johnny somehow managed to play his usual trick of allowing his opponent to take a massive lead with just a few holes to go. It left his supporters scratching their heads in dismay. By the 12th Bond was in the commanding position of being five up with just seven to play. Those who knew Johnny well would think that he had a secret switch which he could flick on demand and bring him back to life at the eleventh hour, for all of a sudden the golfing giant began to wake from his slumbers. Within no time he had pulled two holes back. He was still in with a chance. However, having raised the hopes of so many, frustratingly he soon felt it time for another nap! He now lay three down with three to play. He finally had no choice. It was wake up or walk out.

A tee shot played to within just a few feet of the flag at the next suggested he could still pull it back. It was enough to send Bond running scared, causing him to pitch in a greenside bunker. Like a rabbit frozen in the headlights, his game just went to pieces. By the time both players walked to the 19th tee there could only be one winner. Johnny would finally prevail but only by the skin of his teeth.

In the semi-final he had no problems dispatching his new opponent, Eric Hambro and by the following day he would be up against Abe Mitchell in the finals. A talented amateur from Sussex, Mitchell was more than 25 years Johnny's junior and would prove a distinctly different proposition to those he had faced earlier. Johnny would need to be wise to his game and to his exceptional length off the tee.

By the following morning the elements had turned in Johnny's favour. The wind had picked up and the clouds were unleashing their worst. Westward Ho is an unforgiving place when the wild weather sweeps in off the sea. On days like these only the hardy survive. There is literally nowhere to hide.

Youth and length off the tee favoured Mitchell, experience and superior technique pointed to Johnny. Few though anticipated another outside factor – the taunts of the crowd. Throughout the early stages of the match a group of venomous spectators had proceeded to pour vitriolic comments in Johnny's direction whilst applauding the play of Mitchell. Little did they know that rather than putting him off, their behaviour would only help to harden his resolve. He may have been two down but that was nothing to the seven times champion. At the 14th he found the perfect opportunity to rise above the animosity. Mitchell had struck a tee shot which looked bound for the safety of the green, only for it to ricochet off a spectator's umbrella into a greenside bunker, an unfortunate but not untypical rub of the green that appeared to have worked in Johnny's favour. On seeing the incident Johnny quickly offered his opponent the chance to play another. Mitchell thanked him but declined his offer. The virulent spectators had no riposte to this sportsmanlike offer and the taunts were finally silenced. The game would be played in the spirit it deserved. Mitchell managed a half and by the mid-way stage he fully warranted his three hole lead. Time to regroup, dry out and take stock.

The opening holes at Westward Ho face straight into the wind. Mitchell now had the advantage with his superior length off the tee. To counter, Johnny drove the ball hard and low. By the 3rd his trusty cleek had played its magic once more. He had pulled one back. By the end of the 15th the match was all square. Time now for some fun on the greens; not Johnny's forte but he liked a challenge. He needed a putt of just a few feet to half the hole, but he faced a major problem. His opponent's ball lay plum on his line. Mitchell had laid him the perfect stymie. Johnny proffered a wry smile in Mitchell's direction. It was recognition that the game had risen to a different level. Johnny's focus was absolute, his precision tuned to perfection. With what seemed like consummate ease, he holed it. The applause of the crowd rang out across the windswept links. On to the next. Two to play. Nothing in it.

And then, in the heat of the battle, on the penultimate hole, a rare mistake from Johnny as he played his second to the distant green. He fell behind again at the crucial moment. By the time both men made it to the 18th green the crowds were lining the final fairway, fifteen deep. Silence fell as Mitchell attempted a four footer for the match, nay the Championship. A standard putt in normal circumstances, but not today. If ever there was a putt to raise the pulse and jangle the nerves this was it. Tantalisingly..... he missed it. His cries of despair were matched by the sighs of the many that now looked on. It was left to Johnny to ram his putt home and they moved to the 19th.

Oh how the momentum can swing to and fro. Johnny was up, Mitchell was down. Somehow Mitchell rallied and they halved yet again. On to the 38th[th] and Johnny played true and straight. Mitchell, excruciatingly, was straight but not true. He was to falter at the final hurdle. After topping his drive, his recovery from the ditch rebounded to strike him on the foot. As a result he incurred a two-shot penalty from which he would never recover. It was a sad way to bow out and an unfortunate way for a match to dwindle and fade, but that is the nature of the game. Not all championships are won and lost by miraculous shots that please the crowds. Despite the lacklustre finish it was nonetheless victory for Johnny who had now won a remarkable eight championships.

It was a long and tortuous train journey for the champion as he headed back to Hoylake. By the time his train left Birkenhead Central station on its final leg home, his carriage was full and people began to recognise the star that was in their midst. Two of his fellow passengers were en route to join in the celebrations at Hoylake station and yet here was the very man they had come to see, sitting in front of them. His praises were now being sung and he was forced into polite conversation. To a small degree he was flattered by their kind words of congratulation but he didn't find it easy. There was nowhere to hide. As the train pulled into Meols station Johnny briefly gave his excuses, picked up his bags and stepped out into the corridor. He needed fresh air and some space.

Five minutes later as the train stopped at Hoylake station, he was nowhere to be seen. His fellow passengers searched through the carriage but to no avail. Incredibly, on hearing the news of the impending reception party awaiting him, he had got off one stop early and had decided to walk home along the beach. The hundreds of supporters waiting at Hoylake were dumbfounded by his absence as were Jack and his sisters who were also awaiting his arrival.

It was typical of Johnny. He hated the fuss but there was to be no escape. As word got out the crowds just headed for the hotel. Within minutes of Johnny's arrival, Jack and Elisabeth had returned to the hotel to meet him but there would be words said.

Nagged by his sister Johnny would be forced to make an impromptu speech to thank his loyal fans at the front of the hotel. They responded with spontaneous applause and he greeted them with sincere thanks for their loyalty. As he turned away and headed inside, the scene in the main hotel bar was very much the same. A large reception party was expectant and waiting, determined to praise him to the rafters whether he liked it or not.

Behind all the strong words, Elisabeth was delighted at her brother's latest success. Even she had never dreamt that he could bring home yet another title when most of his generation were succumbing to the fitter and bolder talents of youth. Johnny had long since beaten previous records of major wins, but this was an incredible achievement for a man who was now 50 years of age.

~

Two years later Johnny travelled to Royal St. George's in Kent. It would be the last time that players assembled for a major tournament before war broke out in 1914. Johnny never seriously contended but the trip was notable for an incident that encapsulated the very essence of the man.

Johnny had been out practising with three of his old playing partners: 'Guppy' Cairnes from Northern Ireland, Sidney Fry, the champion billiards player and Robert Harris, the man who Johnny had defeated on the 19th only a few years back in the 1910 quarter-finals.

On the 3rd hole Johnny sliced his ball into a devilish pot bunker beside the green. Harris being one to enjoy the odd joke was still trying to persuade Johnny of the benefits of using a niblick[14]. This was an extremely shallow-faced club that players had been using to coax balls out of difficult lies in bunkers. Johnny had for years despised the club, calling it an 'evil spade'. His solution, which he had mastered most ably throughout his career, had been to use a much steeper-faced club, but to open the face and slide it under the ball. More often or not this worked well but on the odd occasion

---

[14] The niblick was the modern day equivalent of a wedge or a nine iron.

it failed spectacularly, leaving him shame-faced and with the ball still resting at his feet.

Harris passed Johnny the niblick. It took a while but somehow with much reluctance, he was finally persuaded to use it. The result was perfection. With the strange club in the magician's hand he swung it back with nonchalant ease and floated the ball effortlessly over the bunker's edge before dropping it silently into the hole. The roars of laughter that erupted from his three onlookers were deafening. Johnny was embarrassed beyond words. The jibes went on for months afterwards. If only he had used this club sooner how many more championships could he have won? John Ball was a stickler in his ways and a perfectionist in his play but the stubborn man had been hoisted by his own petard that day.

MR. JOHN BALL, JUNR.

John Ball
circa 1899

Thomas Owen Potter looks on as Johnny's father, John Ball Senior practises his putting. In the background is The Royal Hotel.

Ball tees off at the 7th hole at the 1899 Amateur Championship at Prestwick

Freddie Tait's career was tragically cut short whilst fighting in the Boer War

Ball faces off with G. C. Wighan in the semi-final.

Outside the clubhouse at Prestwick prior to his victory in the final

Robert Maxwell drives as Ball watches on in a Scotland versus England
challenge match

John Ball, the first amateur to
win the Open Championship
and now, in 1912, the eight-time
amateur champion.

# The War Years

By the start of 1914 heavy clouds of despair had descended on Europe. By June the assassination of Arch Duke Ferdinand of Austria had triggered the start of 'the war to end all wars'. It was one that would lead to the cruel and shameful loss of many millions of lives..

At first the mood of the nation was buoyant and upbeat. The tens of thousands of men who enlisted each month were confident that the war would be over by Christmas. They were determined and excited at the prospect of defeating an enemy, which in their view was fighting a most evil and unjust war.

No one could ever have foreseen how long the conflict would last or the true extent of the vast casualties that the country would endure. Johnny had witnessed suffering in South Africa that few could ever imagine and he remained despondent at the news he was hearing. Like others who had fought in the Boer War he had a sense of foreboding of how future events might unfold.

Each day as he made his way over to the farm, the fairways of his home course remained deserted. Play was suspended. The nation was at war and golf was a pastime that was superfluous to present day life. There was no will, no support for it. Club competitions ceased to exist as did national championships. It would have been an insult to all those who were fighting the cause, to have staged them. In addition men simply weren't around to play the game.

For fear of offending anyone, Johnny kept his practice to a minimum but when he did, he took himself well out of sight to a discreet corner of one of his fields. He couldn't live life completely without his golf. It was part of his very being. Back in the hotel business was sparse. A few regulars kept the tills ringing but everyone's thoughts were with those who were marching off to war.

Across the country the many new recruits departed for the front, accompanied by the cheers and tears of their anxious loved ones left behind on the railway platforms. The reality of it all was brought even closer to home as two of Jack's sons, John and James, were amongst those heading to the western front. Both were signed to the Kings Liverpool Regiment. They had no choice when the order was sent. It was a worrying time for Jack. Little did they know what would be awaiting them. In many ways it was best they didn't. Johnny did, at least in small measure. He was only glad that his age was against him but he was seriously worried for Jack and his two sons.

Sadly on the morning of 19st October 1916 his concerns were realised in the worst possible way. Johnny needed to call in to the clubhouse. He had taken his normal route, cutting across the course and continuing round the back of the 18th green to the building's entrance. To his right the distant hills of North Wales loomed larger than normal. Dark, threatening skies signalled heavy rain on the way. Johnny was keen to seek the shelter of the clubhouse before the deluge came. Inside, the gas lights would normally be burning bright; Harold Janion would be working away at his desk, Jack tinkering away in his workshop or swapping the odd tale with the senior members. The club provided a strong social function for its members. Even if golf was not being played few of the club's stalwarts would want to miss out on the local gossip. The main bar room would normally be a hive of activity but not this morning. Today there was hardly a soul around; not even the cleaning ladies chattering amongst themselves as they attempted to bring some kind of order by clearing up after the previous night's entertainments.

Johnny walked on past the bar and out through the back door. Jack's workshop was at the top of the building. Johnny looked up but it was in total darkness. The Royal Liverpool Flag stood at half-mast. This could only mean one thing. From the very early days of the war he had been dreading this moment.

A few minutes later he was at Jack's door. The expression on his friend's face told him all he needed to know. Jack's son, John, had been killed in action in France, aged just 29. The telegram had arrived that morning. His father was distraught. As Jack showed him the written news Johnny hugged him as he would a brother. John Morris had gone to fight but no one thought it would end this way. Jack had never prepared himself for this. Why would he? In amongst the propaganda there was little mention of this side of the war. In the months to come there would be no visit from any army officer, no other official contact, just a parcel which arrived through the post containing John's personal possessions; his bible, a bronze vesta case and a photo of him with his family. These possessions were all his father and mother had now, apart from their memories.

Jack avoided the golf club over the next few months. He had no wish to share his grief with anyone there, preferring to remain within the comfort of his family. He prayed every night for his younger son James from whom they had heard no news since Christmas.

Johnny did all he could to comfort Jack over the next few months but he felt no real purpose in his life here in Hoylake any more. Playing golf was out of the question. It held no relevance to him for now and he was becoming tired of putting in the hours out in the fields. In truth he needed a change.

~

Johnny had never been especially close to Katherine, the youngest of his sisters but time had slowly drawn them together. She was married now and had had a son, Lawrence. Along with her husband Oscar, they were now living across the Dee Estuary, in North Wales. Johnny had got to know Oscar well and their friendship grew to the point where they bought a property together in Lygan-y-Wern near Holywell. The house, a large Georgian building, needed some work, but Johnny soon used his talents to make the repairs that were necessary. The property came with four acres of land, enough for Johnny to raise some mares, a few donkeys, and to have chickens in the back yard. In time he would become almost self-sufficient. He would employ a housekeeper, Nellie. It was an ideal arrangement that worked well for them all. With regret he decided to terminate his lease on the farm land in Hoylake. For the time being he could still survive financially by keeping a share in the hotel. Elisabeth still lived and worked there but they agreed to appoint a new manager, Muriel

Robinson, to continue to run the business in Johnny's absence.

The remaining war years would prove tough in more ways than one for Johnny. Jack's loss had brought back memories that had been buried for so long. Sadly they resurfaced yet again on the news of the death of Jack's remaining son James, who would also die in action just a year before the end of the war. On the night the armistice was struck, there were few celebrations in the Morris or Ball household.

# Rise of a New Star

By the time golf returned to British shores a wave of fresh new talent had arrived on the scene. Francis Ouimet's success in the 1913 US Open as a young nineteen year old, had taken the golfing world by storm. He was the first amateur to win the US title, just as Johnny had been the first to win the British Open. He would succeed against all the odds at the expense of the established and respected English professionals, Vardon and Ray. As an unknown, amateur rooky from Massachusetts, Ouimet had just bucked the establishment. In the land of the free where success favoured the bold and the brave, anything was now possible if you had the spirit, talent and determination to make it happen. His success would encourage more and more American wannabies to try their luck across the pond on British soil. Amongst them was a fresh-faced, soon to be Law graduate from Atlanta, Robert T Jones.

Bobby Jones wasn't new to the game. He had won his first competition at the tender age of six, and encouraged by his father, he would soon develop a technique that few could rival. He would also benefit immensely from having the chance to tour his home nation to play in regular tournaments and exhibition matches during the war years at a time when British players were being denied the same opportunity. Across the United Kingdom courses were being requisitioned as valuable army training camps as part of the essential war effort. Golf literally ceased to exist.

Conversely, in the States, Jones was gradually honing his game and building his skills to take on the world's best. Even more impressive was the fact that he was doing all this, not as a professional, but as an amateur.

By the time the war ended Jones's talent needed testing on the global stage. However Britain was still reeling from a war that had caused the loss of millions of lives. Slowly, very slowly the nation recovered and with it came a desire for normality once more. Golfers took to the fairways and enthusiasm for the game returned.

At the end of April 1921 a team of eight American amateurs including Bobby Jones and Francis Ouimet, set sail from New York to Liverpool. They were bound for Hoylake.

A fortnight before the Amateur Championship commenced, they would challenge their British counterparts, nation versus nation, to a contest which would later take on far greater significance. By now Johnny was well past his prime. It was seven years since he had played in any real competitive sense in championship play. He was 59 years of age. He couldn't be considered for the British team but he could still act as a willing supporter. Also present in the crowd was Harold Hilton. No spectator could claim to have greater knowledge of the American game than he. Winner of their Amateur Championship eight years previously, he was keen to see how the American game had progressed.

A severe drought in the run-up to the match had left the Hoylake fairways parched and brown. The conditions were an eye-opener to many but wisely the Americans had arrived early to ensure they fully acclimatised. Along with some essential sightseeing, they would put in many hours of practice on the bold, running fairways. Few rated their chances, perhaps firmly of the belief that Britain was bound to prevail. In the end the home nation failed spectacularly. They were trounced 9-3 on home soil. Bobby Jones was amongst the many Americans to win, and to win well. Despite the result, the overall contest would be a resounding success to such an extent that the President of the United States Golfing Association (USGA) announced that he would donate a trophy for next year's matches. From now on it would be competed for on a biannual basis, the venue alternating between British and American soils. It would be named after the President of the USGA himself and would be called the Walker Cup.

Having achieved his first goal, Bobby Jones moved on to his next: the up and coming Amateur Championship. Johnny would also compete. It would be the last time he would do so in any serious way. He progressed well enough but eventually succumbed in the 5th round. Much that the local support may have been behind Johnny, the world's attention was now focussed on the young American talent. Bobby Jones was adapting well to the dry conditions and was pulling a strong following. Back home in the States the reporters had a field day in the first round when they heard he was drawn against a local player named Hamlet. It played into their stereotyped view of Englishmen, (although naïvely they ignored the fact that he was in fact Welsh). In true fashion the game followed the bard's script. Neither player covered themselves in any glory.

Bobby soon made things worse by allowing his volatile temper to affect his game. In the end it was a lucky break that saw him through to the next round, his ball taking a welcome ricochet off Hamlet's to win him the match at the last. Johnny and Harold had made their way in amongst the crowds to get an insider's view for themselves. They had completed their rounds a few hours earlier. Initial impressions left them unimpressed. However their opinions soon changed. Bobby sailed through the next few rounds, comfortably seeing off his competitors with displays of magnificent golf. By the time he met his next opponent his magic dust seemed to have vanished. After initially being three down within the first four holes, he had briefly rallied before finally losing to Allan Graham by the decisive margin of 6 and 5. Despite his loss his play bore many similarities to Johnny's when he was much the same age. Like Johnny, Bobby would also go on to bigger and better things. This contest would eventually be won by the Scot, Willie Hunter, but along with the team match only a few days earlier, these weeks would be remembered for the debut on British soil of a rising American star.

Two weeks later Bobby's reputation had become somewhat tarnished. After progressing well in his first few rounds, he had picked up his ball in a fit of temper in the penultimate round of The Open at St. Andrews – a cardinal sin for which he would have to atone. The youngster had unquestionable talent but his etiquette needed to improve. Back home in his new residence in North Wales, Johnny reflected on the occasion when he too had visited St. Andrews as a young 23 year old. Likewise baffled by the unusual natural design of the course and irked by his bad play, he had similarly broken the unwritten rules of golf and had walked off the course without handing in his card.

Despite all the initial criticism of Bobby's actions, Johnny could empathise with the American.

It seemed eminently fitting that in 1927 both Johnny Ball and Harold Hilton should compete for the last time in the Amateur Championship at their home course at Hoylake. Each man was attempting to achieve his one hundredth win in the competition. Sadly it was a goal that neither would achieve although Hilton did progress through to the fourth round.

By now Johnny was 65 but this still wouldn't stop him from thrilling the crowds for one final time. He was still able to show flashes of his old brilliance. A low trademark cleek at the 4th to within a few feet of the flag was the pick of the bunch and at the 14th at 5 down he rallied his supporters once again by winning the next two holes with ease, including two superb shots to the 16th green. Ultimately though all good things must come to an end and Britain's greatest and most loved amateur golfer would finally bow out on a course where he had learnt to master his trade as a youngster all those years ago.

Johnny's golfing career may have come to an end but that of another was beginning to flourish. Bobby Jones was rewriting the record books. One British Open, two US Amateurs and two US Opens were already under his belt by the time the British Open returned to St. Andrews in 1927, but it wasn't only his play that was receiving praise. An incident which had taken place in the 1925 US Open had now established him as the man with implacable honesty and integrity. He had declared a penalty on himself after causing his ball to move a fraction at address even though no-one else had seen it. Despite being asked at the end of his round whether he still wanted to sign for a score that included his self-inflicted penalty he wouldn't back down. Incredibly, he would go on to lose the Championship by just a single stroke for being, as some suggested, 'just too honest.' Bobby never saw it that way but simply retorted that, 'you might just as well praise me for not robbing a bank.' The man's integrity was beyond question and the public would love him for it.

This time around at St. Andrews, he would go on to win The British Open by a massive six shots. His resounding victory had helped to change his mind about a course which he had openly stated his dislike to in 1921. In his acceptance speech he asked endearingly that, 'the trophy should be left with his friends at St. Andrews.' It was through these words and deeds that the Scots would finally take him back into their hearts. It was almost exactly twenty years ago to the day since Johnny Ball had likewise been accepted into the welcoming arms of the St. Andrews faithful. He too, had had his previous differences with this famous old links but he had also made amends. The two great amateurs had much in common.

# Meeting with an Old Friend

It was soon after Harry Vardon competed in the 1928 Open at Muirfield that Johnny decided to renew his friendship with the six time Open Champion by inviting him to spend a few days at his new home at Lygan-y-Wern. The two had kept in regular contact over the last few years and their friendship had grown stronger as a result.

Johnny was astute enough to know how Harry might be feeling on nearing the end of his playing career and considered that a few days away might be just what he needed. Having just missed the cut at The Open, Harry was beginning to feel that competitive golf might be best left to the youngsters but that didn't mean golf couldn't still be played at a social level. It was therefore unsurprising that a few rounds were to be on their agenda during their time together.

The years were catching up on them both but hardly a day passed without a swing of the club and the crack of iron on ball. Could either truly retire? They were certainly bowing out with a degree of grace and elegance. These qualities after all, had been hallmarks of their play throughout their respective careers.

Harry had set up a highly successful golf manufacturing business in his later years. This, combined with the publication of a series of sought-after instructional books on the game, had ensured he wouldn't want for money as he moved into retirement. An exceptional golfing talent combined with a keen business sense was a recipe that had brought him significant financial reward.

For Johnny, as one who had played the game in the amateur world, success had brought different rewards. He had been proud of his golfing achievements but his successes had extended well beyond the fairways. He had been equally at home working the land, in tilling the fields, and making his living from his farm. It was this just as much as his golf which had been the mark of his life although few would have seen it that way. He had taken over a run-down business and had turned it around. He had grown up an artisan in every sense of the word and had made a fine job of it. Johnny had been happy with his lot and he wanted for little. And so it was that the two gentlemen would meet and would renew a firm and respectful friendship that went beyond their common sporting lives.

Johnny had arranged for a car to meet Harry from the station at Flint. It was a mere fifteen minute journey from here up the tight, winding roads of the Halkyn hills to his home. He would choose Holywell Golf club on which to play their rounds. He was well known to all at the club there and was always afforded a special welcome. Few though recognised his compatriot when they arrived and the two were happy to be left alone to enjoy their few hours together.

'What will it be then Johnny – a shilling a hole?'

'Are you trying to turn me into a professional Harry,' came the reply.

The remark drew a chuckle from his opponent.

'A shilling it is then.'

The two still retained that competitive edge and by the 5th it was clear that each was inspiring the other as first one ball and then the other, landed within just a few feet of the flag.

'On you Harry.'

The six-time Open Champion had faced many of these short putts and he would not be fazed by this one. In it went, swiftly followed by Johnny's.

'No sign of nerves there Johnny.'

'Nothing but pride riding on that one, Harry, but I've missed a few in my time I can tell you. You know I've used every club in the bag to putt with during my career and they're just as missable even with the finest of all wooden Vardon putters as with a driver I can tell you.'

In truth, putting had been the weakest part of the game for both champions. Harry, in particular had struggled when the effects of his tuberculosis had left his hands trembling and fighting for control at the time when he desired steadiness the most.

The converse was the case when driving however, and as the holes progressed it was clear that neither had lost the timing and the effortless finesse that had enabled both to become the most accurate players in the professional and amateur games. By the time the two approached the 15th the wind had got up and was full in their faces. Johnny was up first and drilled a low cleek into its teeth, the ball barely rising more than twenty feet above the ground.

'That's a John Ball shot if ever I saw one.'

'Driving a ball just the right height for the day, Harry, that's all. It's served me well enough over the years,' came the reply.

In executing his shot Harry saw the play very differently. Taking an extra two clubs to counteract the strength of the wind, he struck his ball clean and true, merely grazing the turf in front of him as he did so. The result was a shot which rose much higher than Johnny's but one which deviated not a fraction in flight, neither left nor right. Both balls would end up side by side in the very centre of the fairway. By now the club professional had cottoned on to the royalty that was present on his course and had sneaked out to watch from the back of the 9th tee. Their tee shots were accompanied by hearty applause. What Bernard Darwin, the eloquent sports writer would have said if he had been in the presence of these two great players together, one can only imagine. He was once quoted as saying of Johnny that,

'I have derived greater aesthetic and emotional pleasure from watching John Ball than from any other spectacle in the game.' Praise indeed.

Of Harry Vardon he was to say,

'I do not think anyone who saw him play in his prime will disagree as to this, that a greater genius is inconceivable.'[15]

Neither of the two gentlemen could quite conjure up the consistency in their games that they once had, but there were more than a few flashes of brilliance that few could have matched.

---

[15] Bernard Darwin was the Sports correspondent for The Times for almost fifty years and was a fine amateur golfer in his own right. In his day he was the voice of golf and waxed lyrical in his admiration for the play of John Ball and latterly Harry Vardon. He spoke of these two in his book 1944 book, 'Golf between the wars'.

And the result of their endeavours? Well, in the end no money changed hands and they retired to the clubhouse.

After a couple of ales and some hot soup the two settled down by the fire in the corner of the lounge bar.

'No regrets then Johnny?'

'Few my friend. Perhaps one? Back in '95', it would have been, at St. Andrews. That second to the 19th. Why, oh why I played that spade, I don't know. Confound that club. It should never have been invented. If a man can't learn to play a shot into the wind, well he shouldn't be allowed on the links. I wasn't thinking. I just picked up the club on a whim and dumped it in the burn.'

'We've all done it Johnny. You won't be the first or the last but you got there in the end at St. Andrews all those years later, that's what counts. Beat them on their home course. They don't like that, the Scots.'

The two men had played at such a high level for so many years that they had numerous tales to tell. A warm fire, a few whiskies and two leather armchairs made for a comfortable evening. The following morning they would play one more round before Harry returned south to his Hertfordshire home.

# The Greatest Challenge of them all

Over the next few years there was much talk of how good Bobby Jones had become. He had the smoothest, most elegant of swings. He also had the modesty and the calmness in adversity to beat the best. He had now done so on countless occasions. It was to his credit that all his successes had been achieved as an Amateur whilst still juggling his responsibilities at work. The similarities to a certain John Ball were uncanny but he was now taking the game to another level. By the time the American public were welcoming in the New Year of January 1930, the rumours were rife that Bobby had set himself one final goal, to attempt what had never been achieved in the history of the game, to win all four majors – The British Amateur, The British Open, The US Open and The US Amateur in the very same year. It would be a phenomenal achievement if he managed to pull it off. The physical challenge would be immense. The mental challenge and the strain on the nerves would be even greater.

In May 1930, Bobby Jones set sail for England, on the Mauretania, a first class liner befitting of a man of his well respected status. He left America in the grip of crisis. The Wall Street crash of October 1929 saw a country reeling and the effects would send shock waves throughout Europe. The Great Depression had begun and America was desperate for a hero to lighten the gloom. Bobby Jones arrived with the nation's hopes planted firmly upon his shoulders.

He would start his campaign with The British Amateur at St. Andrews in late May and entered the contest in fine form. Only a few weeks earlier he had been part of the American team which had defeated the British in the Walker Cup at Royal St. George's. Once play commenced in the Amateur he got off to a flying start. In the first round he completed the first four holes in just twelve shots, even holing from a bunker in two at the fourth. He would go on to beat Syd Roper on the 16th. After coasting through the following few rounds, next to fall in a nail-biting contest would be the bold and talented Cyril Tolley. Harrison Johnston, Eric Fiddian and George Voigt were all subsequently dismissed to set up a 36 hole final against R.H. Wethered the following day. In the end Bobby would come away as the comfortable winner, on paper at least, by 7 and 6, but it had been a hard and strenuous affair. In his acceptance speech he was to say that, 'I felt St. Andrews had been good to me when I was lucky enough to win the Open Championship but I wish to say now that the winning of the Amateur Championship Cup has made me happier than winning any other cup in the past.'

Comparisons of Bobby's achievements with Johnny's successes were heightened when the press picked up on the fact that the next contest up, The Open, would be played at Johnny's home course of Hoylake.

Johnny had no intention of missing this one, be it this time only as a spectator. He had arrived from North Wales to stay in The Royal Hotel a few days earlier and was pleased to welcome some good friends to stay as guests. Harry Vardon, J.H. Taylor, Ted Ray and Bernard Darwin, were just a few of the renowned golfers and journalists to have booked rooms and all were keen to witness what could turn out to be history in the making. The last and only time a golfer had held the Open and Amateur titles at the same time was almost exactly forty years ago to the day. The man to have done so had also won eight Amateur titles in the process. He was the very owner of the hotel in which they were staying.

Seventeen years ago J.H. Taylor himself had won the Open Championship here in 1913, a year when the winds had blown fiercer than ever before. He was now the holder of five Open Championships. Ted Ray, the tall, bold Englishman was likewise a past Open Champion, winning in 1912. He had subsequently gone one step further by winning the US Open in 1920 whilst touring the States with Harry Vardon. However it was Mr. Vardon himself who could feel most proud. He topped them all with six Open titles under his belt. There was some fine golfing pedigree staying at The Royal Hotel.

Needless to say the bars were full the evening before the first day's play and the talk was keen as to whether anyone could better Bobby's seeming mastery of the game. He had easily come through the qualifying rounds but disappointingly almost half the Americans had been eliminated. Only eight now remained to battle it out on the tight, flat expanse of prized open links land at the mouth of the River Dee. It was good news for the Brits who were feeling battered and bruised having seen their trophy take up almost permanent residency in the States for the last six years. Oh, how they longed for a Vardon, Taylor or Ball of old.

Strangely it was almost exactly 10 years ago that Vardon and Jones had lined up alongside one another in the 1920 US Open at The Inverness Country Club. At the time Jones was a fresh faced 18 year old and was playing alongside his hero in his first ever US Open. He was just starting out on his career back then, whilst ironically Vardon was taking his final curtain call in this, America's most revered championship. Vardon, the 50 year old master, had been the key man to have helped grow the game in the States through his three lengthy tours there in 1900, 1913 and 1920 and Jones had indeed witnessed his prowess in 1913 as an enthusiastic young eleven year old. Seven years later he was to play alongside him in his nation's prized tournament. Over those two opening rounds Vardon had quickly recognised the latent talent that the teenager possessed. Now 10 years on at the point of making history at Hoylake, he was keen to see whether the mature 28 year old could now fulfil his promise and succeed when the pressure was at its most intense.

Only a small minority of the large crowd actually saw Bobby tee off on the 1st. Most were craning their necks for a view. They missed a rare, tentative drive which saw him take an early bogey but he would later rally to post a more than respectable 70. He would follow this with a safe 72 in the second round to place himself one shot clear of the Englishman, Fred Robson, at the half way stage.

By the start of the third round the home support was crying out for a brave challenger. It would come in the form of the tall, imposing and brazen Welshman - Archie Compston.

With putts flying in from every angle Johnny was keen to witness events first hand. In his company were the familiar and talented Englishmen, Harry Vardon and Ted Ray. By the time they reached the players three more early birdies from Compston on the back nine had got the crowds believing a home win might be possible.

'He could do it you know, Harry,' Johnny whispered.

'I'm not convinced Johnny. But can you notice any similarities to a certain gentleman not too far away?'

Taking his pipe from his lips, Harry looked across to Ted Ray next to him.

'You're right. What do you think Ted? He's got that same swashbuckling style about him as you. Drives the ball a country mile as well. That's you alright. Give him a trade mark hat and that's Ted Ray of old, on the charge.'

The comment deserved a reaction from the big man and he got it. It was simple and most apt. In one single movement Ted inclined his head in Harry's direction and with suitable deliberation he raised his hat in appreciation of the remark.

'Thank you my man,' he replied.

Harry interjected, 'But here's the rub Ted. Is he going to win it?'

'If he's anything like me Harry, he'll blow it that's for sure,' came Ted's reply.

'Never!'

The three shared the good joke and moved on.

Could he indeed do it? As it turned out, by the end of Compston's round he had posted a new course record and he would take the lead going into the afternoon's final lap.

After a good meal back at the hotel it would be Johnny who would be out early to see the final showdown at first hand. This time Elisabeth had joined him and with her arm tucked in his, together they made their way out to the far end of the course. Following play at a discreet distance but with a sturdy pair of binoculars slung round his neck was Bernard Darwin, the renowned Times sports correspondent. He looked on intently, notebook in hand.

Bobby took advantage from a stroke of good luck on the 2nd when a ball bounced off a spectator's head to leave him with a clean lie in a bunker when the alternative would have been far worse. He was the first to check that the spectator wasn't badly injured. It was a reflection of his true character that he seemed more distressed by the incident than the spectator was himself. Taking advantage of his good fortune he played his bunker shot with consummate ease and holed the putt for a birdie. Calmly he kept his game on track until the 8th. The hole was a comparatively simple affair, a straight if long par five. He had played it well for the first two rounds, and after his initial two approach shots there was little to suggest he shouldn't do so again. He now lay just thirty yards out and was eyeing up a potential birdie. Somehow he managed a double bogey seven. Bobby cursed his careless play. By the side of the green Johnny and Elisabeth looked on in disbelief, not quite comprehending what they had just witnessed. Back down the field Compston had blown up but Bobby wasn't aware of the fact. Surely he couldn't do the same, could he, not in his final hour?

Johnny knew the feeling only too well. He too felt the pain and the agony Bobby was going through but he was powerless to help. He had followed his career from afar for a long time. Somehow this talented star just had to find that last ounce of energy and determination to succeed.

Despite the setback, Bobby would hold himself together and slowly, one by one, the few remaining challengers fell by the wayside.

Strangely, few spectators surrounded the green on the 18th as Bobby finished. Most were expecting others to pip him at the last. Johnny was there to see the final putt but it was too early to say whether his play would yet be good enough. There were still a few to finish.

In the end it was.

As Bobby was presented with the trophy, he had just enough energy for a brief but modest speech and finally, he retired to the ultimate safety of the clubhouse.

# Two Modest Men, Two Golfing Greats

Johnny was keen to get back home to North Wales after the events of the championship but he still had one task to perform. It might be a while now before he returned to the club and he was keen to tie up a few loose ends. He couldn't leave without saying his farewells to the staff in the clubhouse. They had been so good to him over the years. He wanted no fuss. He never did; just a quick thank you and good bye.

Most of the crowds had left by now. It had been a long day; an exciting day and even Johnny had been moved by the scenes he had observed and by the play of the new champion. Bobby Jones was a man Hoylake had taken to its heart in almost the same way they had to Johnny himself all those years ago. He was worshipped in his homeland and he was pretty popular here too. Remarkably he was half way to achieving the greatest feat in golfing history. Would he do it? Only time would tell.

Johnny was hoping to find one of his old friends in the clubhouse, Joe Marshall. Joe was one of the two loyal employees who had worked for him as a labourer on his farm all those years ago. After Johnny's move to North Wales he had put in a good word for Joe at the club and they had taken him on as a steward. The two men went back a long way. Joe would normally be in the locker room after events like today. He would usually be busying himself with tidying away all the mess left behind by the players. He was meticulous in his approach, to the extent that within a few hours of any tournament finishing, the locker rooms would be as pristine as if no one had been present all day. Unusually Joe was nowhere to be seen and the locker room, still distinctly untidy, was almost vacant but for a smart young gentleman clearing away his clubs in the corner. Johnny had barely noticed him as he entered but as he turned to leave, the gentleman smiled briefly in his direction. Johnny was stopped in his stride by his familiar face. In an instant he realised who it was.

'Excuse me sir. Are you Mr. Jones?'

'I am. Is that Mr. Ball?'

'Yes it is.'

'I am truly honoured to meet you Mr. Jones. Can I offer my sincere congratulations on your magnificent victory this afternoon?'

'Thank you Mr. Ball.'

'But please call me Bobby.'

'And do call me Johnny.'

Their handshake was warm and long.

'Please be assured the honour is all mine, Mr. Ball. There is no one in golfing history who has achieved what you have; to have been the first amateur to win the British Open and to have done so in the very same year as also winning the coveted Amateur title – a unique achievement. You have set the standard for all to follow. I doubt anyone will ever achieve the haul of amateur titles that you have.'

'You've done the same now Mr. Jones and more besides. My successes are little compared to yours, especially given the pressure and the expectation you are under. Since retiring from the game I have followed your progress. I do believe you can win those two remaining titles before the year is out, that is, if your mind is set to do so. Your talent is unmatched.'

'I am tired though. Every hole, every stroke, it drains me. If I can summon up the energy I will give it my best shot.'

'I understand how you feel. There are few who would know what it truly takes to win at such a high level. I was certainly successful but it is you who carry the torch for all amateur golfers today. Your play, your style, your successes; they are unrivalled.'

For the next half hour the two Champions swapped tales in the clubhouse and the smiles never left their faces. Each was equally pleased to have finally met the other. They continued to address one another by their formal titles despite their introductions. In the end Bobby had to leave but not before one final gesture from Johnny.

'I have something here which I would like you to have, Mr. Jones. It was given to me years ago by a very special player. As a keen student of the game you will know of him. His name was Young Tom Morris, the greatest golfer of his day. He became the proud owner of the esteemed Championship belt, the forerunner of the Claret Jug which you now have in your possession. He gave this to me when I was just seven years old. I had planned to donate it to the club but it seems more fitting that it should be in your possession now.'

Reaching deep into his pocket he took out the treasured golf ball given to him almost 60 years ago. Silently he placed it in Bobby's hand.

'It has been a true honour meeting you Mr. Jones. I wouldn't have missed your play for the world.'

# Epilogue

Johnny was quite content living out his final years in his country home at Lygan-y-Wern. He still made the occasional return trip to his spiritual home in Hoylake.

Oscar, Katherine and their son Lawrence would in time move away, giving Johnny the opportunity to buy the property outright. Soon after, Elisabeth, Johnny's older sister, moved in. It was a major move for her, having lived all her life at The Royal Hotel. Johnny and Elisabeth had been close all their lives but sadly this was soon to change. As time passed, Johnny's friendship with his housekeeper, Nellie, grew stronger. They fell in love and finally married at Holywell Magistrates office in 1932. The marriage sadly caused a rift in Johnny's and Elisabeth's relationship.

Johnny died at his home in 1940 leaving nearly all his estate to Nellie. Only two of his golf medals still exist. These he left to The Royal Liverpool Golf Club. Visitors can still see them to this day. The rest he gave away to friends.

As for Bobby Jones' golfing achievements and the future of Amateur golf, many will know that he did go on to win both the US Open and US Amateur Championships by the end of the year. In doing so, he made sporting history by winning all four Major Championships in the same year – 'the impregnable quadrilateral'. The feat has never been equalled and it is unlikely that it ever will. Like John Ball he would also be awarded honorary membership of the Royal and Ancient Golf Club of St. Andrews.

# EPILOGUE

Bobby Jones is rightfully heralded as the world's greatest ever amateur golfer but John Ball must run him a very close second. He is without doubt Britain's greatest amateur golfer. His final tally of eight Amateur Championships and an Open Championship is unlikely to be beaten. He will forever be remembered as the first amateur to win the Open. Had he lived his life in the modern era he would likely have courted the same status and prestige of a Nicklaus, Palmer, Ballesteros or Woods, but he would never have wanted it. Remarkably only three amateurs have ever won an Open Championship, two of those being members of The Royal Liverpool Golf Club: Harold Hilton and John Ball. The third, Bobby Jones also has strong connections with the club. It was at Hoylake that he first played golf in Britain and it was here that he won the second part of his quadrilateral. Soon after his achievement he was granted honorary membership.

It was The Royal Liverpool Golf Club which first inaugurated the Amateur Championship back in 1885 and it was the instigator of what later became known as the Walker Cup. When this prestigious competition returns once again to Hoylake in 2019, John Ball's achievements will be rightfully commemorated as the club celebrates its 150th anniversary.

# John Ball's Major Victories

1888 The Amateur Championship, 5 & 4 Johnny Laidlay, (Prestwick Links)

1890 The Amateur Championship, 4 & 3 Johnny Laidlay, (Hoylake Links)

1890 The Open Championship, 164 shots, won by 3 strokes, (Prestwick Links)

1892 The Amateur Championship, 3 & 1 Harold Hilton, (Prestwick Links)

1894 The Amateur Championship, 1 up Samuel Mure Fergusson, (Hoylake Links)

1899 The Amateur Championship, 37th hole Frederick Tait, (St. Georges Links)

1907 The Amateur Championship, 6 & 4 C. A. Palmer, (St. Andrews Links)

1910 The Amateur Championship, 10 & 9 Colin Aylmer, (Hoylake Links)

1912 The Amateur Championship, 38 holes Abe Mitchell, (Westward Ho Links)

A total of eight Amateur Championships and one Open Championship victory

The Irish Amateur Championship 1893, 1894, 1899

The St. George's Challenge Cup 1888, 1889, 1890, 1891

# Bibliography

A History of Golf, Robert Browning 1955, A & C Black Publishers

A Journey through the Annals of Golf 1888-1910, H.R.J. Grant & D.M. Wilson 2011, Grant Books

Bobby Jones and the price of glory, Curt Sampson 2005, Holtzbrinck publishers

Golf, Bernard Darwin 1954, Burke Publishing

Golf and Golfers, Horace Hutchinson 1899, Longmans Green and Company

Golf between Two wars, Bernard Darwin 1944, Chatto and Windus

Golf in the making, Ian T. Henderson & David I.Stirk 1979, Henderson and Stirk Publishers Ltd

Green Memories, Bernard Darwin 1928, Hodder and Stoughton

Harold Hilton his Golfing Life and Times, John LB Garcia 1982, Grant Books

Hoylake and the 1894 Amateur Championship, B.T Bell & D.I. Hamilton 2001, Grant Books

John Ball of Hoylake, John Behrend 1989, Grant Books

Mighty Winds... Mighty Champions The official history of The Royal Liverpool Golf Club, Joe Pinnington 2006, Guy Woodland

Out of the rough, Bernard Darwin 1938, Chapman and Hall

Royal Liverpool Golf Club Annual Magazine 2017, 2016, 2005

Royal Liverpool Golf Club Scrapbooks 1870 -1912

Sixty Years of Golf, Robert Harris 1953, Batchworth Press

The Amateur, The story of the Amateur Golf Championship, John Behrend 1985, Grant Books

The Daily Telegraph Golf Chronicle, Ted Barrett 1994, Carlton Books

The Glasgow Herald Newspapers 1870 – 1910 online source

The Grand Slam, Mark Frost 2004, Time Warner Books

The Royal Liverpool Golf Club, a history, Guy Farrar 1933, Birkenhead Willmer Brothers & Co Ltd

The Tempest of 1894 and its sequel, the story of The Royal Liverpool Village Play 1895 – 1995,  John Spence 1995

Tommy's Honour, Kevin Cook 2007, Harper Sport

West Kirby and Hilbre, J Brownbill, 1928, Young and Sons

# Acknowledgements

Writing a biographical novel which depicts the life of a man whose major achievements date back over a century, is not a perfect science. The author has a clear responsibility to ensure that he tells his story in a way which is as accurate as possible according to the historical facts available to him, but that it is also told in a way which keeps the reader entertained and engaged throughout. A deliberate decision was therefore made to use dialogue as this was felt to be the best way of portraying the characters as they were likely to have been. Before doing so every effort was made to ensure all available sources were used to discover their true nature and to explore how John Ball lived his life.

Considerable research was undertaken to help in the planning of the novel. In particular John Behrend's, 'John Ball of Hoylake' is a superbly written book and provided a wealth of material.

Other valuable sources included Guy Farrar's 'The Royal Liverpool Golf Club,' Joe Pinnington's, 'Mighty Winds... Mighty Champions', and Robert Harris', 'Sixty years of Golf'. The Glasgow Herald proved an especially valuable source giving blow by blow accounts of golfing action during tournament play and it was crucial in revealing that Old Tom Morris was present at many of the Amateur Championships in which John Ball played. His close family connection to Jack Morris, through his brother George, and his admiration for John Ball's play provided key evidence to establishing the friendship between the two fine golfers.

I am indebted to the diligence of Thomas Owen Potter, the early Secretary to The Royal Liverpool Golf Club for assimilating the many cuttings from newspaper reports of the time. The smell of history as one turns the pages of the thick leather volumes in which they are bound takes one instantly back to those halcyon, early golfing days.

There are some events within the novel where a degree of artistic licence has been taken but that is the nature of an historical novel. Did John Ball indeed pass his treasured golf ball on to Bobby Jones? ...well it is fun to dream.

Particular thanks are due to The Royal Liverpool Golf Club's Secretary Simon Newland and to his staff for allowing me access to the rich treasure trove of golfing history contained within the club's library. Without their help Hoylake Hero would never have got off the ground.

Others who have given of their time to support me and to whom special thanks are due include: Joe Pinnington, Anthony Shone, Bob Grant and Neil Alveston.

However my greatest thanks go to my partner Marianthi, for her artwork in the book's cover design and for her patience and perseverance in the seemingly endless editing process. Her support and encouragement throughout has been immense. Johnny may have been Hoylake's hero but she will forever be mine.